# Unload Email Overload

# Unload Email Overload

How to Master Email Communications,
Unload Email Overload and
Save Your Precious Time!

By
Bob O'Hare
MSc, BSEE

Executive Coach
Corporate Change Agent

BALBOA.
PRESS
A DIVISION OF HAY HOUSE

ISBN: 978-1-4525-5224-8 (sc)
ISBN: 978-1-4525-5226-2 (e)
ISBN: 978-1-4525-5225-5 (hc)

Library of Congress Control Number: 2012909488

Balboa Press books may be ordered through booksellers or by contacting:

Balboa Press
A Division of Hay House
1663 Liberty Drive
Bloomington, IN 47403
www.balboapress.com
1-(877) 407-4847

Printed in the United States of America

Balboa Press rev. date: 10/29/2012

# Dedication

I dedicate this book to you, the reader, and to the thousands of individuals all over the world who are suffering the burden of email overload, receiving hundreds of questionable emails every day and losing countless hours of your lives trying to keep up. Here's to you and your newfound freedom.

I dedicate this book to you, the corporate executive, who feels the pain of productivity loss due to social networking, Smartphone technology, information overload and email distraction. I wrote chapter eight for you.

# Contents

# Preface

Out of college with an engineering degree, I changed vacuum tubes the size of 12-ounce water bottles to repair the Univac II, one of the earliest electronic computers. I later developed and sold communication terminals so computer users could interface directly with computer power. In 1976, at Digilog Corporation, when computers were still physically large and communication terminals were connected to computers through acoustic couplers at 130 bits per second, I developed the concept of a small, low-cost, fully integrated desktop computer. We used CP-M software, the predecessor to MS-DOS, and one of Intel's early integrated circuit processors, the 8080. It was one of the first personal computers.

I tell you this this because I am proud to have participated in the development of digital technology, which has revolutionized global communications. People and organizations can connect and communicate quickly, cheaply and more effectively. Digital technology has made the world a smaller, better place.

My attention now is focused on the proliferation of Smartphone technology, tablets and iPads, social networking, email communications and information overload.

I conducted a short survey of my own with my coaching clients and business acquaintances to determine for myself if there was enough evidence to justify writing this book. The 30 responses mirrored what had been revealed to me in extensive studies by others. To begin with, the sheer volume of email, with its attendant carbon copies and convoluted history threads, is excessive and getting worse, gobbling up precious time while often accomplishing nothing. Workers are treating email as a priority that has to be dealt with immediately, at the expense of the work they are being paid to do. The ever-present Smartphone and the desire to be connected all the time has become stressful, costly, disruptive and a detriment to maintaining a healthy balance between work and life.

In short, email, a great communication tool, is being relied upon disproportionately to the increasing exclusion of other communications tools, such as the telephone and one-on-one conversations; and it's being managed ineffectively, which further contributes to information overload and the experience of email as a burden.

Many people may blog an idea or two about resolving the issue. Good for them! It helps all of us. My approach, a little different, has been to develop a methodology which, when practiced, will change behavior, help achieve the best value from email communications and reduce email overload. This book presents that methodology, MasteringEmail™—the twelve principles, the processes and then the details—without tying my work to a specific email system like Outlook, Gmail or Lotus Notes.

I developed MasteringEmail™ to help you get your job done without constant email interruption and the pressure of an overflowing inbox. I also expect it to improve your work/life balance, reduce your stress and help you recoup time you should be spending with friends and family.

Thanks for coming along.

# Acknowledgments

I'm grateful to those who helped me prove that my quest was worthwhile, responded to my surveys and helped me zero in on the book title and subtitle.

I deeply appreciate the advice, input and challenges I received from Stu Halasz and Robert Curwin. Robert and Stu made great suggestions for my early work.

Thank you to Terry Frediani, Mimi Urgovitch and Tina Hennessey. You read my early manuscripts and got me underway.

Heartfelt thanks to Ann McHale for reorganizing the material and providing the first real edit. Nice job, Ann; thank you for your love, time, and effort.

Ashlee Hall, Rodrigo Brinski, Scott Hendrickson and Fred Livezey helped me develop my marketing tools and social network—what a job that was!

David Morgan, a real professional in creative arts, critiqued the book covers and provided significant refinements.

And, in the end game, Marguerite Del Giudice took control and did a marvelous job turning my work into a real book. Heartfelt thanks, Marguerite.

I depended on my wife, Carol, for counsel, support and motivation to complete this project. Thank you, Carol; you have always been there for me.

# Introduction

As nearly every one of us has a computer on our desk at home and at work, email enables us to communicate next door or around the globe in seconds. On a personal basis, we can share with others, receive and search for information and stay connected with friends and relatives. Email is quick and easy. There is no paper and there are no stamps. We don't have to run to the post office and we have immediate delivery. Some people believe email and overnight delivery services will put the United States Postal Service out of business.

On October 8, 2011, Martin Bryant, European editor of *The Next Web*, wrote an article stating that the first email message was sent in October of 1971. He also noted how email was really embraced twenty years later when the World Wide Web went public.

Email is a great communication tool; however, it raises significant challenges. For many knowledge workers, managers and busy people, email has become a distraction and a burden that raises anxiety and steals personal time. As a consultant and executive coach, I'm always hearing complaints about email overload—hundreds of emails in the inbox, some there for over a year. In one recent case, over four years; wow.

The headline article in the money section of *USA Today* on May 18, 2011, was entitled "Distractions for Workers Add Up: Technology Can Actually Reduce Productivity." According to the survey of 515 white-collar workers by Harmon.ie, a social software provider, distractions caused by social media, email and badly designed office technology may cost a company with 1,000 workers ten million dollars a year. The study concluded that more than half the workers wasted an hour or more per day on interruptions, with 60 percent of the distraction due to electronic devices and email.

When we started working together, one client had 1,200 emails in his inbox and assured me he needed every one. We started a dialogue about what needed to be there and why. He began to agree it would be better to file or process the email as soon as possible rather than leave it for later. In 30 days, he was down to 500 emails, determined to see that inbox empty. Another client started with 600 emails in her inbox; with some effort, we got it down to 200. Then she discovered the crux of her problem: She wanted her employees to send her carbon copies of every email during their training period. She never saw the tipping point where they were trained and they thought she just didn't trust them. Clearing up that misunderstanding significantly reduced the amount of email she received.

Clients, and those I have surveyed, say they can't escape the onslaught of messages throughout the day. When finally, at the end of each day, they are free to process all the messages, they stay late at work or process messages at the dinner table. Clearly they're receiving too many and suffer from information overload, and they allow email alerts to add to their stress by keeping their Smartphones on all the time.

I hear computers and personal devices gonging and buzzing during meetings. I watch people acknowledge incoming email during our one-on-one meetings, and I've seen people play with their Smartphones, on their laps, during group meetings. You can call it multitasking. But recent research indicates that multitasking is a myth: You cannot pay attention in a meeting and process email at the same time. You can only flip back and forth, tuning into one thing at a time, like switching between television channels; you get the overall picture only by filling in your own details, which may or may not be accurate. At a business meeting, a multitasker could miss something important or be embarrassed if called upon—have you been there?

In some occupations, history threads within emails can be useful—for continuity, numerical data or foreign-language words. However, I've seen email with long and confusing history threads, sometimes created for purposes of self-defense or self-protection. Other threads are created by hitting Reply to All without thinking about it first. I have heard complaints about the time it takes to sort out threaded messages, the unnecessary people added to the distribution list and the frequent changes of subject. Confusing threads cause disruption and anxiety.

How about carbon copies? Individuals are afraid to quickly delete carbon copies for fear they might miss something; so they read them and then become frustrated by the time it took, without any benefit. Not knowing what to do with a cc, many people just leave it in their inbox, only to be distracted every time they see it. And of course they add up and bog you down.

With Smartphone technology, email is just that gong away. Many knowledge workers with an always-on mentality respond each time a message arrives, an interruption that interferes with the business at hand, meeting participation and concentration. This then happens at home and the kids' soccer games as well.

There is also texting. The young woman who plowed into the rear of my car while I was stopped at a traffic light was texting. An accident ready to happen was driving next to me on the Pennsylvania turnpike with both fists on the wheel and both thumbs on the Smartphone—and the women had a child in the car.

Suffice it to say, many individuals, socially, want to be connected all the time. The Smartphone revolution has led to social pressure to be always *on,* always *connected*, making it difficult for us to just shut off our devices. There is often pressure from your company also. If your handheld is on while you are driving and an email or text alerts you, what do you do? Discipline yourself, please. Don't reach for the device to take a look. That is really dangerous. In fact, if you are driving, shut the thing off. Receiving a text or email alert in a conference room or meeting is not dangerous; however, it does distract you, and fumbling around with your machine is distracting for others.

I believe these problems are compounded because most people do not process email effectively. They look at it, ponder, partially process it, and leave the email in the inbox to consider again later. Their full inboxes create confusion, they miss deadlines, their replies don't fit the subject and they have inbox anxiety. Well, sure! Most of us were never trained to process email. We learned by the seat of our pants.

Basex, a knowledge economy research and advisory firm headquartered in the New York City area, published studies stating employees and managers see email as a big part of the information overload problem and that, ironically, the same individuals contribute to the excessive volume of email flowing through the system. Basex has developed a tool to let organizations estimate what information overload may cost them. Visit www.iocalculator. com or www.Basex.com for more information or to give it a try.

My own email survey and references in the media have verified my observations about email overload. Cody Burke, a senior analyst at Basex, involved with an ongoing survey about information overload, released a research brief on February 10, 2011, entitled "Cody Burke, Information Overload." At that time, in the study, email—with 66 percent of the votes—was perceived to be the greatest cause of information overload. Clearly, going home relaxed at night requires getting email under control. Cody's brief is at:

basexblog.com/2011/02/10/more-information-io.)

I believe email processing time can be reduced significantly when distraction, confusion, interruption, cover-your-rear-end-thinking and poor messages are replaced with well-thought-out email messages and intelligent use of the media. From now on, consider email to be a communications medium like regular mail and don't expect an immediate response. Don't let email replace face-to-face dialogue and telephone conversations. It doesn't make a lot of sense to send questions and answers back and forth in a string of emails. Pick up the phone more or converse over lunch.

Many key employees have told me they would just like to go home to their families and not worry about urgent business messages on personal time. Here is the question: What is *urgent* and in whose mind? If a company, or your team, developed a mutual understanding about sending and responding to urgent messages, I'm sure fewer urgent emails would be sent at night or on weekends.

There has been some buzz about banning email altogether and, instead, using social networking to communicate. The idea, I guess, is to blame email for being the cause of information overload, interruption and a negative effect on individual productivity. Well, I agree, there is too much email, and, by managing email ineffectively, a person can be interrupted frequently by incoming email and lose concentration on the work at hand. With no email there can't be email overload; that's clear. However, I don't see yet how substituting social networking can solve the problem.

One could suggest we chat electronically instead. That's immediate, or frustrating when you expect it to be immediate and nobody responds. If you are available and someone wants to chat, that interrupts you, no? A chat has its advantages; however, you don't have time to think, as you would with an email inquiry. You will blab your reply, hoping it is intelligible, without regard for accuracy, clarity and tone. Then what's said is out there. Chatting also doesn't work when several time zones are involved. So, no, I don't think electronic chatting will solve any overload problem.

How about we set up a central database? When I want your help, I'll write a note, put it in your online folder and hope you check your folder before I miss my deadline. Suppose I need to know something about a team project. I can assume one of my team members put the information in the central database. But where—under the project name, his name, my name? Finding that info could take some time and I could get sidetracked if I found something interesting to read. So, no, I don't see how a central database will replace email.

Social networking may help some of us once it's evolved more over time, but for now my mission is to help you unload the overload by teaching you a better way to do email, the MasteringEmail™ methodology.

MasteringEmail™ is predicated on the assumption that email is not a schedule, a ToDo list, a document file or a document pile. It's a plan that will save you from scrolling up and down through a cumbersome, stale inbox, searching for what you fear you might have forgotten to do. Ideally, at the end of each day, I would like you to have your email fully processed, your inbox empty, your mind clear and relaxed, and your life in balance.

The straightforward and intelligent methodology of MasteringEmail™ will benefit you in the following ways.

1. You will not be a slave to arriving email.

2. You will have fewer disruptions.

3. You will feel less email frustration.

4. Processing email will take less time.

5. Email will help you plan, organize and control your work.

6. You will write effective email messages and send fewer carbon copies.

7. You will make better choices: email, phone or meeting.

8. You will maintain a near-empty inbox.

9. You will have time to think, create and improve decision-making.

10. You will be and feel more productive.

11. Email will steal less personal time.

12. There will be no email overload.

To make progress quickly, scan the book first. When you see a MasteringEmail™ idea that makes sense to you, try it right away.

As a team leader or team member, I suggest that you develop team email etiquette. Agree on email processing times that meet global requirements and account for time zones. Set turnaround and reply expectations. Come to consensus on the use of carbon copies and threaded histories. Decide when not to use email communications, and determine circumstances for using the telephone, conference calls, text or personal contact instead.

If you are a member of upper management, hold a position of higher authority or have a broad sphere of influence in your organization, you will find interesting ideas to ponder in Chapter Eight, Exploring Productivity: A Guide for Managers.

Bob O'Hare
Philadelphia, Pennsylvania
October 2012

# One

# Principles

This chapter provides you with the underlying principles of MasteringEmail. It will show you how to relieve the anxiety of email overload by spending less time processing messages and more time doing actual work. In addition, your colleagues will benefit by your example, and your life will get easier as they follow your lead, making for a healthier work/life balance for everyone. Imagine the joy!

Principle 1 **Maintain separate work and personal mailboxes**

Create two email addresses, one for personal email and one for business email. Large organizations require that you do this for a good reason: They know that the availability of personal email will distract you from the job you are being paid to do.

Spending time on pictures, jokes and personal matters robs your focus and can distract your colleagues, especially if you forward to them. On the job, paying attention to business is what's ethical and courteous. Personal email, perusing the web, and having fun on the computer are best done when you are not on company time. Redirect personal email to your personal account—better, let your assistant do this, if you have one—and explicitly ask friends to use your personal account for personal email. In a short time, this change alone can significantly reduce the number of emails arriving in your office inbox.

### Principle 2  **Do not surrender today's plans to today's email**

Don't think of incoming email as a spontaneous ToDo list, unless it's your job to respond immediately to incoming email. Instead, discipline yourself to use your email to build a task list, arrange your calendar and organize your work. The way to save yourself from surrendering today's plans to today's email is to plan your work and work your plan. That way, you should be able to get your work done and go home at a reasonable hour.

Email sent or received today should only be important to your near future. If input is required for today's work, pick up the phone.

### Principle 3  **Use administrative assistance**

If you are fortunate enough to have an administrative assistant, have your assistant make a pass through your email before you do. A well-briefed assistant can monitor your incoming email more frequently than you can, and—simply by putting articles and proposals into a reading file and forwarding emails you would normally delegate to others—can help coworkers get on with business, eliminate junk from your queue, and prevent you from becoming the bottleneck. *This is a big one; start today.* Your assistant, according to your instructions, can then leave in your inbox only important items upon which you must take action. Personal assistants are smart and understand what is important to you. Discuss how you would like to work together. Listen to them. Trust them! They will like that.

Most upper-level managers do have administrative assistants that review and process their email. If this is the case, when writing to them, do not carbon copy their assistants. Telling this to your people can eliminate hundreds of carbon copies.

Principle 4   **Batch process email by appointment with yourself**

This principle, in particular, is essential to managing your email effectively and relieving overload.

If receiving and responding to email is your job, as in customer or technical service, each arriving email is a priority that requires your full attention. But for most of you, this is not the case. Email is just a communication tool, not a priority and not meant for immediate reply. That being so, it is best to ignore arriving email and evaluate it in context with other communications, such as telephone calls, memos and face-to-face meetings—just one business task to perform among all others. When it comes to email, *make appointments with yourself to process email and, during that appointment, do nothing else.* This principle will stop email from managing you and stop you from constantly checking your email. Acting on each email as it arrives will only complicate your life. Discipline yourself. Turn off the email alert on your Smartphone, and process email only when you plan to do so.

Let your colleagues and team members know that you plan to process your email at scheduled times each day. Tell them not to expect a reply for perhaps a day. Suggest, in cases of emergency or urgency, that they phone you. By all means have such a discussion with your boss and agree mutually on a plan. Setting expectations will reduce any criticism that might come your way for being non-responsive and accrue credit to you for using your time wisely.

### Principle 5  **Process email last in, first serve**

Process email last in, first serve rather than first in, first serve—let the last email you receive be the first one you process. Last in, first serve makes more sense because it can eliminate unnecessary work. Your inbox might contain two or three sequential emails sent to you over time. The last email might say forget about the first two emails. If you process your inbox first in, first serve, you could end up responding to email that no longer requires a response. Last in, first serve can save you from wasting time and, maybe, appearing foolish. You learned this technique in your first management course, remember?

### Principle 6  **Make three deliberate passes**

As you batch process your email, you will find that messages can be handled effectively with a quick scan through your inbox followed by two specific passes. During the scan, look for very important email—from the boss, surprises and anything requiring immediate input for you to move forward with top priorities. During the first pass, remove all distractions and act on the items your colleagues need from you in order to get on with their work. Process each email one time and remove it from your inbox. Save email requiring more thought and detail for the second pass—work planning, updating your calendar and scheduling time for your priorities, tasks and obligations.

Principle 7 **Delete aggressively**

When processing email during your scheduled times, delete aggressively! Delete carbon copies, threaded email, information that would be nice to know or you think you might like to have some time in the future. And after taking appropriate action on any particular item, delete that email. Do not leave the email there to look at again. Your daily goal should be to *empty the inbox.*

If you see something important, pick up the phone, or make a note to discuss it at the next scheduled meeting. If you feel you just can't delete, ugh, drag it to a folder.

Don't even think about forwarding the occasional "send to ten friends" email; just zap it. You'll be doing them a kindness.

Principle 8 **Send very few carbon copies**

To reduce the volume of email you send and receive, minimize the use of carbon copies. If you want the receiver to take action, put their name on the To line. Send a carbon? Ask yourself if it's really necessary to keep all those people in the loop. Do they need that information, would they want it, or would they be better off without it? Everyone benefits by reducing the hundreds of carbon copies floating through the system, so send a carbon only when you must. In an interview with the *New York Times*, the CEO of Henkel, in Germany, revealed that he deletes carbon copies. If he can do it, you surely can.

Some carbon copies come from colleagues who are actually crying out for help, seeking protection, living in fear of missing something or afraid of doing the wrong thing. If you sense this, reach out and take the opportunity to help.

### Principle 9  **Send less email**

Don't burden your colleagues and managers. Put discussion items on meeting agendas, talk to people in the halls and pick up the phone. *Feel confident and make independent decisions.* Think about whether the email you're sending is important and something the person actually needs to know. Think three times before you send an FYI. Do they have the information already, are you sending it to meet their needs or yours, and is there a better way or better time? People often leave FYI email languishing in their inboxes until they can figure what to do with it, creating bothersome clutter.

Be thoughtful about hitting Reply to All. Are you extending an unnecessary thread? Should you change the subject of a threaded email? Do you want to inform everyone, or do you want just one person to take action?

Imagine for a moment that each time a person opened an email from you, it cost you a dollar, and it also cost the receiver a dollar. You want to know that the email has value to the receiver before you send it so that it's worth your effort to produce it. Thinking of value, you might send fewer emails, resulting in fewer emails for the world to process and far less confusion.

### Principle 10  **Cut the thread**

After receiving an email, you can choose the option to send the contents of that email on to others when you hit Reply or Forward. That's good; it helps the original sender to remember what they said and gives those to which it is forwarded a little background. However, if this option is used several times in a row and copied to various people, the message can develop a convoluted history string. Don't continue a thread if it is not productive or if the subject of the matter has changed. Instead, cut unnecessary information, change the Subject line or take the time to write a new, clear, targeted message.

### Principle 11  **Empty your inbox every day**

*This principle is a must.* When you process email, during your scheduled times, take complete and appropriate action on each email, one by one, and then remove the email from your inbox. Delete it, process it, file it, whatever; make sure it leaves the inbox. Be ruthless.

### Principle 12  **Shut off, or ignore, email alerts**

Do not interrupt one-on-one meetings to read or respond to your email. Smartphones, or visible PC screens, buzz, blink and vibrate. Responding to them is impolite and disruptive and devalues your one-on-one time. Be disciplined. Your temptation to look will be eliminated—and you will earn respect from others for your consideration and for setting a proper tone—if you simply shut off the beep, get away from the PC screen and tuck your Smartphone away.

If you are in an informal meeting and waiting for an important email related to priority work, keep your Smartphone on vibrate, and extend the courtesy of letting others know that you may be briefly interrupted. Otherwise, be courteous and attentive to what is at hand, and shut your system down. Take the lead and others may follow.

During formal meetings, turn off your email or email-notification setting. When you allocate blocks of time to process email, as you would a block of time for a priority task, you will look at email when you plan to, rather than when each message arrives. You will also be able to give your full attention to the meeting. You won't miss anything, will be ready if called upon and will avoid possible embarrassment. You also won't have to send one more email to a colleague asking what you missed.

There you go!

One last thought: *Tell others what you are doing and why.* We sometimes become so involved communicating indirectly by email that we miss something basic and fail to get across essential ideas. When it comes to the workplace, it makes common sense and is mannerly to simply let your colleagues and managers know how you are managing your email, and therefore your availability.

A short, group MasteringEmail training session would be ideal and go a long way toward everyone operating on the same page—and maybe even getting home in time for dinner.

# Two

# Processing Method

When you get home from work at night, you probably check your physical mailbox for whatever was delivered by your mailman. You were not fretting all day over what might be there, were you? Your incoming mail did not drive your actions and decision-making, did it?

So let's think for a minute about how you handle paper mail that comes to your house. Imagine the routine. You open your mailbox, or pick it up from the floor if yours is delivered through a slot, and you go through the pile. First, you scan for anything that looks important or interesting. Advertisement, junk, junk, bill, post card. Ah, a post card. You stop flipping and read it—nice!—then start flipping again. Junk, flyer, bill, bill, magazine, letter response to a job application. You put the pile down and take an immediate action, open the letter and enjoy the good news. Then you resume and finish your scan.

Next, you start sorting. All the junk mail goes together for recycling. Magazines and catalogs are put aside to read later, and maybe you walk over and replace the outdated magazine on your coffee table with the current issue. You put bills in one pile to pay later and the solicitation from the insurance company in a pile of things to research when you have time. There is the one letter addressed to a neighbor, so you make a quick call to say you'll drop it off later. Sound familiar?

Now, some people sit down and write a check as soon as they receive a bill; others put them in a batch for later. You might like to open each bill, toss extraneous inserts, put a return address and stamp on the return envelope and slide the ready-to-pay bill into a binder with other bills. The envelope the bill came in goes in the recycling pile.

Note that the original pile of mail has been sorted and processed, none of the original pile remains and your mailbox is empty. One thing you don't do, for sure, is return empty envelopes, junk mail, piles and bills to your mailbox, which would quickly get clogged up with useless paper. You processed your mail as if you had an appointment to do so. You emptied the mailbox and, essentially, you sorted your mail into three categories: respond right away, dispatch quickly, and plan to work on it.

To manage your email effectively, all you have to do is process it the same way you process your paper mail, during a specific time—an appointment—set aside to do that and nothing else. Your goal for each email is to read and comprehend it, take complete and appropriate action and *delete it from your inbox*. An appointment enables you to process your email according to a plan. If you don't follow a plan, your continually arriving email, instead of you, will insidiously become the driving force of your day.

Begin changing your habits today. Make an appointment with yourself, someplace you won't be disturbed. At your office, use your PC; the convenience of a full screen and keyboard, proximity to your files/folders, and simple access to your calendar will speed the process up. Afterwards, *shut down the email program,* and get on with your work.

How often must you check your email? Start with three appointments a day with yourself as you figure out what works best for you. Check your email when you arrive at work to see what happened overnight; take another look around lunchtime for what happened in the morning; and dive in once more before going home to see what took place in the afternoon that you might have to deal with the next day. That should take 1½ hours a day, maximum. It may take more at first, until the principles start working for you, and you might find that other times of day work better. Just make sure the time you set aside is undisturbed time. Or, you might have to use your Smartphone without the benefit of nearby office conveniences, in which case you just do the best you can. But if you find yourself spending three or four hours a day processing email when that is not your primary job, you are way off target—wasting time, adding pressure, and compromising both your performance and your personal life.

Some people believe you shouldn't look at your email first thing in the morning, because it might derail you from your plan for the day or hijack your priorities. That's a legitimate concern; however, you are not in business alone. What if something happened overnight, perhaps in a different time zone, that requires a change in plans—a customer asking to move a deadline up or back, say? Maybe requirements for a proposal change. In that case, preparing the proposal based on the old requirements would be a wasted effort.

As an alternative, if you know that reading email first thing *would* throw you off, you could plan your next day carefully the night before, after processing your last batch of email. In the morning, do what you planned for the first

11

hour or two before checking your inbox. The main thing is not to let email, which will arrive continuously throughout the day, become your spontaneous ToDo list. Email is for communications. You are supposed to manage it; it should not manage you, and your priority cannot be to automatically respond to the needs of others, unless that is your job. That said, of course be mindful of responding to colleagues or others who can't move forward with their own work until they hear from you. Speedily responding to a half-dozen messages in the morning, when called for, helps keep the larger organizational machine chugging along. It's like directing traffic: You go here. You go there. Wait. Slow down. Back up. Stop. With these kinds of messages, you want to get in, quickly, help others and get on with your day. You have your own agenda, and you owe it to yourself to do what you're being paid to do, and in the time frame you're being paid to do it.

To get started, try my recommendation of batch processing your email three times per day. I've found that works for most people; make adjustments and customize after you've learned a few things and experienced some benefits. To summarize, there are essentially three categories of email—critical, short response, put aside for later—and they are best managed by doing *a quick scan through your inbox followed by two specific passes*. In other words, go through the inbox as you would your mailbox at home. During the scan, look for important messages: from the boss, surprises and those requiring your input in order for you to move forward. During the first pass, 1) remove anything irrelevant to work, and 2) answer straightforward requests from colleagues needing to hear from you to get on with their work. Process each email one time, and remove it from your inbox.

During the second pass, you're addressing items requiring some thought and detail, such as work-planning, updating your calendar, and scheduling time for your priorities, tasks and obligations.

Good planning and execution tells us to do first things first and not to waste time on the little things. The scan plus two passes may seem to go against that idea; it does not. Employees have to collaborate for projects to get done in a timely fashion. Spending a minute during the first pass to answer a question or give permission could mean the difference between somebody making a deadline or not, or you being blamed for the delay.

## The Scan

During your scan, you may see an urgent request from your boss. If so, stop processing email, do what you have to do to satisfy the request, and return to your email later. Do the same thing if you see a serious surprise. All emails are not created equal, so any time you see critical information that requires immediate action, take it. Then get back to your email processing; maybe sooner, maybe later. The scan helps you *do first things first*. You don't want to continually refer to email throughout the day. If you are expecting important (but not critical) correspondence, discipline yourself to look for it during your next email appointment, only hours away. If you *are* waiting for critical information, ask the source to call or text you.

What if you are always on the lookout for email from your boss, or know your boss expects this? Find a way to have a conversation in which you let the boss know you get an awful lot of email and—to stay organized and focused on actual work projects—you set time aside each day to work on it. You're working, but you might not always be able to respond right away. Ask if the boss can live with that. Get them to agree. Alternatively, if you scan primarily for email from a boss or particular person, you can probably make a rule in your email program to have those emails sit at the top of your inbox. Also, your email program will most likely offer an option to mark certain email with a colored flag.

If you find yourself worrying that something might get past you, fearful that something in an email might intimidate you, or you're concerned about missing something, you need to think through that behavior. Take the time to explore within yourself what or who in the work environment has got you on pins and needles and how to get the answers and support you need. Do not confuse this type of fretting with causing your email problems. These are not email problems, but misplaced fears can create and exacerbate email problems. Be sure to take appropriate care of yourself and find a way to address them.

### The First Pass

The key reason for the first pass is to avoid being a bottleneck in your organization, holding other people up by not responding in a timely way. Typical actions on the first pass would be to read the message considerately and do one of the following.

- Delete

- Reply, to answer a question

- Forward, with a brief action request

- Move the email/attachment to a project, client, or miscellaneous folder

- Reply, giving permission, perhaps adding other addresses

- Delegate with a brief, clear directive

- Print a copy for later review

- Add sender to junk mail list

When you see an email that requires more thought, time for consideration or incorporation into your schedule and priorities, leave that email in the inbox for the second pass.

After you take deliberate action on an email, make sure to remove it from your inbox. I can't stress this enough. Do you understand why you can delete the original email? If you replied or forwarded, you already have a copy in your Sent folder, which is your chronological file. As your system has likely been configured to include the original message with a Reply or a Forward, the copy in your Sent folder will be there to refresh your memory, if necessary.

Therefore, realize that you do have backups and can delete safely from your inbox, thereby relieving much of your overload.

Below are some brief statements that might be useful as you reply or forward during the first pass.

- Please put this on the agenda for our next one-on-one meeting.

- Please take responsibility for this and follow through.

- Please stop by this afternoon to discuss this.

- Please prepare a concise problem statement to review with me.

- Please make an appointment for the team, and bring two solution ideas to discuss.

- In the future, please send personal email to my personal email account—me@someplace.com. Thanks.

15

- Discuss with your team; decide together. I will support you.

Another function of the first pass is to act quickly on non-work-related email. When you receive beautiful pictures, attractive retail offerings, or patriotic messages you would like to read, instruct the sender to use your personal address next time. Before you know it, you won't have to deal with them again. Assign to junk or spam folders any correspondence you don't want, the first time you see it and vigilantly afterwards, and over time you will see far fewer retail advertisements and other unwanted solicitations in your queue.

Drag newsletters, articles and conference brochures to a Read It Later (RIL) folder. Whether you read them later or not, they will be out of sight, out of your inbox and off your mind. Perhaps you can dispatch them on the weekend or on an airplane, like the magazines you would like to read that are stacked on your credenza. Leaving them in your inbox will only force you to think about what to do with them every time you see them; then you have to regain your focus. If you don't take action as quickly and decisively as possible, or simply delete whenever possible, you will keep getting knocked off your square throughout the day. That process, like pondering the unfiled papers on your desk, is a waste of time—and aggravating.

Work-related messages, such as guidelines, product announcements, and minutes and events, will show up from time to time. If relevant to a current priority, hold them for the second pass. If low priority, drag them to your RIL folder or get the essence and delete. Realize that someone else will have this information, if you ever need it.

When you can't decide where to put the darn thing and can't bring yourself to delete it, save it to a Just Gotta Keep It (JGKI) folder for another day. At least it will be out of sight, and you won't keep trying to decide over and over what to do with it, or end up dealing with it at the wrong time. Eventually, you will look in your JGKI folder and delete most of what you find.

## The Second Pass

On the second pass, take action on whatever remains. Work sequentially rather than waste any time deciding which one to handle first. Consider that they are of equal importance. Read and comprehend each email. Move it to a folder, your calendar, a task list or the notepad. Take complete and appropriate action, as required by the email message, to act, arrange, schedule and plan. When finished with the email, *delete it from the inbox*. Here are examples of appropriate actions for the second pass.

- Establish a meeting. Delete the email.

- Put items on your calendar and schedule work. Delete the email.

- Schedule phone calls. Delete the email.

- Make a note to yourself. Delete the email.

- Put items on your task list. Delete the email.

- Walk to another cubicle to discuss. Delete the email.

- Print a handout for a meeting, discussion or boarding pass. Delete the email.

- Move the email and/or attachment to your document files. Delete the email.

At the end of the second pass, your email inbox should be empty. If it isn't, you probably don't know what to do with the few that remain. Again, try to delete them. Can't delete them? Drag them to RIL or JGKI. *Empty the inbox.*

Okay, sometimes it really is hard to deal right away with an email, as you may need information or permission before moving forward on some task. You may be anxious about whatever the email requires, and you might want to keep the email in front of your eyes, as a reminder to get back to it as soon as you have thought through how to respond. In such cases, give yourself some slack. Relax. Leave the email in the inbox and move on for now. Time or information will enable you to clear it out shortly, and obsessing over it will only slow you down. There should be very few of these. Don't worry about them! At the same time, don't let them accumulate. Two days is a sensible limit.

If you're like most people I have worked with, you probably complain about receiving 100 emails a day. You think that's too many; agreed. But if you don't change your own habits, nothing around you will change, and you will continue to feel put upon by the nonstop flow and volume of your email. Here's a way to start turning things around: If you want to receive less email, send less email. No need to say thank you or no problem. Cut down on carbon copies, small talk, FYIs, CYAs, and the endless stream of truly interesting but mainly useless things we can't seem to help sending each other—and let others know when you receive email from them that you would rather not get.

Smartphones, of course, are another pervasive distraction. With your Smartphone on all the time, it is easy to be diverted or disturbed at your desk and in meetings. Recall the survey by Harmon.ie that I mentioned in the introduction. It stated that 60 percent of distractions were caused by electronic devices and email. So, turn off the email alert, or leave the Smartphone in your pocket, turned off or on vibrate. Better still—and you may think this is crazy and impossible—use your Smartphone only when out of the office. In the office, use your PC, telephone and watch. Carry a paper copy of your schedule along with your notebook. Smartphones should help you, not add to your stress. Habitually referring to the calendar on your handheld only adds to your overload.

Seek to find the right balance for yourself. Out of the office, you can use the portability of your Smartphone to dispatch some email, during idle travel time at the airport, for instance. Bedtime and breakfast with the family are not good times to process email. Give your life a break! And for heaven's sake, don't even think about emailing or texting while you're driving home. You may not make it.

# My Personal Notes

------------------------------------------------

I now believe my email related issues are:

Here's what I will do to address them now!

I will suggest the following ideas to others to help us all:

# Three

# Personalizing Your Email Experience

First and foremost, create those two separate email addresses (one for your personal life and one for work). You may even want to have a third address for online subscriptions and marketing lists that result in lots of junk mail—a "throw away" account that can be shut down if it gets out of hand. Otherwise, there are a host of settings that will allow you to control what does and doesn't get into your inbox and how your screen looks so that you can maximize convenience and productivity.

Most corporations, organizations and Internet service providers set up spam filters to remove advertising and pornography sent to large distribution lists. Many retain questionable spam for a short time to give you a chance to look at it, so check your spam folder now and then in case something's there that you want. The email program resident on your computer will offer different junk mail options that include automatically sending it to a junk folder or having it deleted as it arrives. If you direct it to a folder, you can review the contents from time to time to make sure the program is not deleting email you want. There will probably be a this-is-not-junk button to push for items you want to keep; it will move the message back into your inbox and allow future email from that address to be delivered. Set junk mail filtering to a low level at first, and move it up if too much junk gets through. If you poke around your email program menus, you'll see other options, like blocking senders and assigning safe senders.

Your email program will also contain options for what you see on your screen when you open it up. I recommend setting it up so you see three sections: 1) your active email folder, most times your inbox, 2) a reading pane that shows you the contents of highlighted email, and 3) a navigation pane showing your folder list and buttons for important functions like calendar, notes, tasks and contacts.

Arrange the inbox by date and time of arrival with the last email received at the top of the list so that you can process last in, first serve, as discussed before. This way, you won't spend time and effort taking unnecessary action on outdated emails.

In your folder list, you will most likely have a Sent folder and a Deleted folder. If you want to look at an email you just sent or deleted, you will conveniently find it at or near the top of the folder, if it's arranged by date.

Here's something else that will speed up your processing. You want to set the reading pane to display the content of highlighted email in your lists (Inbox, Sent, etc.) so you can read the email without having to open it—one less click and less delay. You can also open attachments directly from there. Situate the reading pane under the list of emails if you can, so you get a wider line to read and, often, can see the whole email without having to scroll. This arrangement allows you to move through your email list using the down arrow key. Many emails are short and may not require action, so you can just read the message in the reading pane and delete. Done! Move purposefully through the list, and avoid replying just to be nice. Your friends and colleagues do not need one more email saying thank you or telling them how helpful they were. Unless of course you know certain people do need that, in which case go ahead. Otherwise, stick to business, take action and delete aggressively.

The navigation pane, which displays your list of file folders, provides one-click access to your calendar, notes, tasks and contacts. You want to see these folders so you can quickly drag and drop emails or attachments into them. Of utmost importance, the navigation pane allows you to immediately convert an email to a task, note or calendar item. In most systems you can left-click on a highlighted email, hold, drag and let go.

You will find that email programs offer a lot of options that most people don't use or maybe even know about. For example: You can usually establish rules to process incoming emails automatically, like directing email from a specific person into a special folder. You should be able to flag email from a person or a place, say your boss, and have that appear at the top of your email list. You can most likely add color, font and size to draw your attention.

The overriding goal is to empty the inbox every time you process it. How do you accomplish this when you want to keep an email or attachment—what's the best place to put it?

As a computer user, you are familiar with creating and saving data files, like Word documents and spreadsheets. You may have files pertaining to legal or financial issues, projects and customers. These documents may be stored on a corporate data-file server, your own personal computer or on a network of individual computers. Now consider email communications. Where do you find the mailboxes? Email, likewise, may be stored on a corporate server, your own computer or on a network. Maybe in a cloud!

Bob O'Hare

Data files stored on an organization's file server are usually subject to size limits. The email administrators also limit the size of your mailbox. They usually have a retention policy and may purge email in mailboxes without notifying the user. They might also "padlock" an individual's mailbox until its size is back within limits. You, as an email communicator, have to address these issues. If mailbox size, purging, retention and lock-up policy are troublesome for you, I recommend that you manage your files and folders on your PC, on your own hard drive, where they won't be subject to email administration rules.

Digressing for the moment from where to file email, let's review why you would want to file an email and/or attachment after taking action and making decisions. There is one reason: after taking action on the email, it no longer belongs in the inbox. But completing your work with an email may also include appropriate filing. You might simply want a chronology of what was sent to whom, when, or a correspondence file for a customer, project or vendor. You may want to gather all reading material into one place so you can peruse it at the airport.

Here's what to do to comply with your organization's email restrictions yet be able to conveniently store and find documents you want to keep.

- Recognize and understand the mailbox folders provided to you by your organization. Study the size and retention rules.

- Set up, on your own computer, a personal data file with file folders for customers, vendors and projects. This file might be in your mail program or with your main document files. In both cases, the information would be stored on the hard drive of your PC, rather than on a corporate mailbox server.

26

- When you want to file something, move the email and/or attachment from your inbox to the appropriate folder. Drag and drop where possible, or use the normal document save function. Knowing where you keep your files, for what reason, with descriptive file names, will enable you to find and open them again when needed.

You will probably find the following folders in your mailbox when you set up an email account on your computer.

*Inbox*—When you open your email program, the program will automatically look to your email server for messages. If you have any, the messages will enter the inbox. When you select Inbox in your folder list, you will see a list of the messages. One message will appear in the reading pane.

*Outbox*—Your outgoing email will pass through this folder on its way to the recipient. If there is a problem, like message size, the unsent message will stay in the outbox so you won't lose it while you sort out the problem.

*Sent*—This folder will fill automatically with emails you send. Consider it a chronological record. Think about this. When you reply or forward, with the original message attached, you can delete the original email in your inbox without losing any information. Sometimes you will want to peek here to jog your memory or drag the sent email to another folder.

*Deleted*—This folder fills as you delete your emails. As with the Sent folder, you will find value in having this available. Every once in a while, whoops; you accidentally delete. You do have to empty this folder periodically or it will cause you to exceed your mailbox size limit.

27

*Drafts*—This is a place for temporary storage, unfinished business or messages you want to sleep on before sending. Be careful not to let an important idea or message get lost in there.

*Junk*—Your email program will automatically establish a junk folder. You will be able to select whether to fill this folder with junk, so you can review it—just to be sure—or, you can choose to let junk be deleted without looking at it.

Here are a few additional folders you could set up on your hard drive to help you empty your inbox.

*Personal*—If you don't have much to file, have not yet arranged for a personal email address or don't see the need for two email addresses, you can drag your personal mail to this folder, so it is out of the way and won't distract you when you are working. You can enjoy the contents later, off the clock. Watch out for temptation; don't let this folder distract you.

*Read It Later (RIL)*—This file is like that pile of papers and magazines on your credenza or the corner of your desk. Handle what's in it the same as you would handle the paper. Actually, do a better job. Read the material in the airport or on a plane. Get what you can from it and then delete it. If you pick up ideas for your staff, take the time to put the idea into your own words and create an email or an agenda item. Think twice about burdening your people with a forwarded email containing the entire article or a link. They will have to file it as RIL because it came from the boss, even if it interferes with their time management. You can be sure they will find, on their own, enough articles to read; don't forward an entire article unless it knocks your socks off.

*JustGottaKeepIt (JGKI)*—If you don't know what to do with the thing in your inbox, don't labor over it very long.

Drag it to JGKI and move on. It will be out of the inbox and out of sight. Maybe you'll benefit from it later. Most likely, you'll zap it the next time you see it. Consider automatically purging anything that sits for 30 days, and set up the purge when you establish the folder.

Let's relate the RIL and JGKI files to good time management and organization principles. Remember the ABC method? At the end of the month, you sort your A, top priority items, and B, second priority items, and you throw all remaining C items in the trash, the idea being that you didn't get to the C item for 30 days and your world is still turning. You didn't need the C items and can guess you don't need them going forward. If you ever do need them, they will come back to you somehow.

Okay! So, at the end of the month, muster the courage to purge RIL and JGKI. Maybe you feel you have to look through them and delete manually; however, I think that is self-defeating. Use your technology to automatically purge RIL and JGKI files on the last day of the month. Bingo! Gone! Never to be missed.

How about those folders you added for customers, vendors and projects? If you believe those folders might get too large, you can create specific ones for each customer, vendor or project. It is even possible to create sub-folders like memos, invoices, shipments and customer relations. Having folders consistent with your work relationships helps you to organize and have the right data available in the right place when you need it. You can drag a pertinent email from the inbox to a folder; then, later, when you're dealing with specific customer issues, you can refer to the folder without having to rummage around in a cluttered inbox searching for the relevant email.

As previously noted, have your folders visible so you can drag and drop an email or attachment conveniently into the appropriate one. If they are visible in your navigation pane, that will work very well. If your folders are with your main documents, then open the list of those folders in another window and adjust the two window sizes so you can see both your email program window and your main document folder window at the same time. To review a filed email or attachment, highlight its folder.

Some people use software filter applications that automatically file email away in appropriate places. If that works for you, okay. For me, it just creates more than one place to look for incoming mail and can raise more concern over what I might have missed. I find that my email program contains all the filters and features I need. If you have an assistant or admin, let them take a crack at filtering your incoming mail. They can filter reading material into the RIL folder and forward email they know you would delegate anyway. They also can turn down meeting requests that they know you would feel guilty doing yourself. Then, all you'll see in your inbox will be your most important work. If your admin misses something, don't worry; key issues or important messages have a way of resurfacing. Without an assistant, I suggest concentrating on email at the time you plan to do so and aggressively deleting messages your inquisitive self would normally take time to process.

Files can get large, old, stale, out of date and beyond legal retention requirements. Some things you save, you probably will never look at again and do not need. When you get used to this methodology and have more discipline, these issues will subside. After you are set up and operating confidently, you can look more into archiving. Your email system will let you archive files automatically or manually, based on rules you establish. If you don't want to keep files after a period of time, they can be deleted. If you want to keep them forever, you can move them to removable storage. Worry about that later.

There are, of course, a number of email systems. I am most familiar with Microsoft Outlook, and, although I've tried to write this book in a generic way, some things I suggest might only work in Outlook. If so, please forgive me. When you want or need to study the functions of your system, you will be able to find all the details you need by searching the Internet for your email system vendor.

To summarize:

- Set up meaningful files and folders—and drag.

- Process email in a batch three times a day.

- Aim for a near-empty inbox every time.

- Keep it simple.

- Leave the next batch time for tomorrow.

- Go home.

- Enjoy your evening.

# Four

# Detailed Inbox Processing

This chapter will explore in greater detail how to make appropriate decisions and get your inbox count to zero just about every time you batch process your email. It includes examples of specific situations you might face and instructions for how to convert an email into a customized item on your ToDo list, a calendar entry, an appointment or a note.

In my observation, many people go on autopilot when doing email. Far too often, they open an email, read it, think about it, and close it without taking action. They have been distracted from what I expect was something more important and have wasted their precious time. Later on, they return to the same old email and repeat the same mental process, except now there are new emails to worry about. Feeling overwhelmed compromises their ability to make decisions.

Because this habit of scrolling through an inbox, looking for something to do and getting nowhere, is an engrained, self-defeating process that can only be broken by practice and persistence, the simple principles of MasteringEmail bear repeating and elaboration. Here we go!

<u>The First Pass Revisited</u>

## Read, phone, delete

You receive an email asking for an explanation of a problem. You know the answer and begin to type a reply. You're three paragraphs in before realizing that so much background is required for your explanation to make sense that you aren't even close to being done; what you had initially thought could be handled with a quick reply would be better addressed in a phone call or a meeting. At that point, immediately stop typing and pick up the phone to find out when the sender can talk. If you don't call the person and just go on autopilot and complete the email, you'll set in motion a very inefficient and draining chain of events whereby you end up spending a lot of time and mental effort composing and proofreading a complex reply, which the person on the other end then has to read and absorb and respond to with inevitable questions, which you will then have to respond to. Keep in mind that email is just one of any number of communication tools available to you. Just because somebody asks you about something in an email doesn't mean you have to answer in an email. In this case, after talking to the person who asked for the explanation, hang up and *delete the email.*

## Read, delete aggressively

You receive an email recounting an animated discussion from a meeting you did not attend. The email is a carbon copy, sent simply to keep you in the loop. You read it and start to reply before realizing that the email was not addressed explicitly to you so why are you getting involved? Resist the urge to put your two cents in, and think of it instead as a serial soap opera. This type of email "conversation" is destined to go back and forth three or four times; you probably will be copied every time; and you know that the players are going to include a long email thread you can tune into later if you have the interest and time. So, in this case, don't get sucked in by the drama; *just delete it.*

### Read, delete

Some emails require no action. An FYI, a thank you, carbon copies informing you and a list of others that a project has been delayed or a milestone met can be deleted. Because you are on the mailing list of people being informed that something has happened, you can assume that you will hear when the project is back on track. So you gain nothing by holding onto what was intended as a quick communication. Such an email is not something you need to frame and hang on a wall. *Delete it.*

### Empty your trash

Delete aggressively! Delete FYI carbon copies and stop thinking that you will throw away something you might need later. For goodness sake, don't file unimportant email. Do you keep an extra trash can at home for trash you might want again? Or do you keep your trash for a couple extra weeks in a "holding area" before putting it out for pick-up? In the rare instance you might need the information you threw away, you can always ask for it from the person who sent it. They (and all the other people on the cc list) will still have a copy. If emptying your trash folder at the end of the day scares you—is the missing silverware in the garbage?—configure your trash folder to delete anything two weeks old. When trash accumulates, you could run out of memory or your administrator could shut you down.

### Read, use threads judiciously

When you reply to a received message, you most likely have the option to include the original message, appended

35

to the bottom. There are cases where it's necessary to remind someone of what they sent you. Many busy (multitasking?) employees and managers with a large span of control and many balls in the air rely on this feature to stay on top of things. Others use threads to maintain legal conversations, foreign words or numerical data. Okay, use it, but be discriminating.

Email conversations can go back and forth for a while, new people may join in along the way, and the subject may change. Long threads can become cumbersome for folks trying to catch up with the whole context or make sure there's no compliance violation. To avoid confusion and including unnecessary information in your reply, create a new email rather than replying to the old one. You can use relevant information from the thread by cutting and pasting it into your new email. You can also cut off early parts of a thread that no longer apply. If the subject changes, change the Subject line. You can also configure your software so it does not automatically append the original message.

There's something else about threads that you need to keep in mind: Email configured to include earlier messages exposes potentially confidential information to eyes you may not have intended to see it.

I once sent an email to a senior VP, to confirm an appointment and provide my agenda for our feedback session with an executive. I meant for the agenda to be between the two of us, it was not meant to be seen by the executive. The VP's admin replied to me that plans had changed and that the VP was going to be out of town. She also carbon-copied the executive and his admin, and, because her system was set up to include the original email, the carbon also included my confidential agenda, thereby alerting the executive to something I did not want him to see; it also inadvertently shared sensitive information with the exec's admin, who did not need to know what was going on with her boss. The lesson for me was to be more careful, perhaps writing "confidential" on the Subject line or sending a private note to the admin. After I discussed the nature of my work with the VP's admin, she decided, in my case, to send new email messages rather than her standard reply containing the original message.

## Read, forward

When you forward a message, and your software is configured properly, the message you forward will appear on the screen with an area for your message above it. To relieve email overload, be thoughtful about what you forward. If you are forwarding an email with a thread, consider deleting the information that is not pertinent to the receiver. Do not start or continue unnecessary threads. And ask yourself if your email will pertain to the same subject that is on the Subject line. If so, the previous subject with the "re:" before it will suffice. But if your message changes the subject, put the new subject on the Subject line. Consider also to whom you are forwarding. Those you want to take action should be listed on the To line, others (not many if any) in the cc box.

You probably have the option in your email program to forward with comments. This option is cool, as it enables you to reply point-by-point to the original email within the actual text of that email, and each insertion can be marked with your name.

## File

When you personalize your email system, you set up folders. You will put some folders in your email box; and, to avoid conflict with email-retention policies, you will locate some folders on your own personal computer that are totally under your control. These folders may relate to a customer, a vendor or a project and can contain any sub-folders you wish to create. So when you need to access information, it won't be buried in a full inbox. When you need it, you will know where to find it quickly.

## Store temporarily

Ideally, as you realize by now, you want to handle each email once, do what you have to do, get the email out of your inbox and move on. But until you have internalized these new habits, you can allow yourself some wiggle room. You can drag an email to RIL. A half-finished email? Put it in Drafts. Don't really want to read it, getting anxious and just can't delete it? Off to wither away in JGKI. You can deal with these temporarily stored messages when you have the time—if ever. Get them out of your inbox.

## Remember one more thing

When you send, reply or forward, a copy of the email is automatically saved in the Sent folder. This is your handy chronological file, dated and available if you need it. But there are issues to consider: How long do you want to keep a record of sent mail? Does it matter how much mailbox space you use? Does your company automatically purge files; if so, how often; and will your email administrator cut off your email if that mailbox gets too full? To limit the size of your files or delete contents periodically so your email administrator doesn't shut you down, check out the archive and auto-archive options available in your email system. If you need a chronological file where you can safely store your correspondence for months or even years, discipline yourself to move files to external storage periodically.

### The Second Pass Revisited

What remains in your inbox will involve managing your time, planning, organizing work and controlling business.

Because there are many email programs, the following instructions may not be exact for you, but they'll put you in the ball park. For more specific instructions, consult your tech support people.

## Task or ToDo list

Instead of making a ToDo note on a Post-It or the back of an envelope, you can simply drag and drop the email to the Task bar or whatever equivalent is in your program for listing tasks. When you let go, the email transforms into a task window for you to complete.

If your new task would likely have the same Subject line as the email, leave it as is; if not, simply modify it to something more meaningful. All the details of the email will remain in the body of the task window, including the time, the date and the person who sent the email. In that window, you will also see space to set a start date and a due date. You can probably set a reminder as well, and a reminder is so much more efficient than scanning an inbox for things that have to be done. You can add notes, ideas and thoughts about the task by typing above the email text, or you can edit down the information in the email while you're thinking about it. You can also include contact information for others who might be involved in the task by selecting it from your address book.

Often, tasks are planned weeks or months in advance, so the more helpful facts you put together now, while you're thinking about it, the easier you'll make it for yourself when the task reminder pops up down the line.

Let's say you have a document on your hard drive that you'll need for this task. The task window probably has an insert function. Look for it. It will allow you to insert the current version of the file and have it open for you in the task window when you need it. If you think you might modify the file between the time you establish the task and time you'll be working on it, look for an option to insert a hyperlink to the file instead. The hyperlink will open the latest version of the file for you. Now, the most important thing for you to do: *Delete the email from your inbox.*

Here is another example. Suppose you are a manager and you received an email suggesting a task you want to delegate to one of your people. Drag and drop the email to the Task bar. As in the previous example, prepare the information needed to start the task, add your instructions and then assign, or delegate, it to the employee. To assign the task, look for an Assign button in the task window, add a name or names and any instructions. To deliver the assignment, press the Send button. The receivers have the option of accepting or rejecting the task and can manage it from their own computer. If you trust them to get it done, you can delete the email from your inbox. You can also look for a reminder option. You can tweak the process based on feedback from the people to whom you are delegating. If you want a task to happen frequently, you can click the Recurrence button in the task window, or its equivalent, and review the available options.

Here's a little story that validates the value of taking the time to learn how to convert emails into detailed task items.

Jim, an engineer, has to build a machine, so he sends a purchase order to Fred, the purchasing agent, for the parts he needs. Jim tells Fred when he must have these parts in order to meet his deadline. Fred formally acknowledges the request, but Jim knows Fred always needs to be reminded. To make sure he receives his material on time, Jim leaves Fred's acknowledgment in his inbox to remind himself to follow up with Fred in a week.

Now, how many times does Jim look at his email each day? Even though MasteringEmail suggests you look at it no more than three times, Jim checks his 20 times a day. By keeping Fred's acknowledgment in his inbox, Jim has to look at it, and then ignore it, twenty times every day. Over the work week, Jim will look at that email 100 times and think, "Oh yes, I have to follow up on that next week; I can ignore it for now." Suppose Jim, who is nervously conscientious about getting things done on time, has five such emails in his inbox that need his follow-up. During the week, Jim will look at these emails 500 times, mentally consider them, however briefly, and then try to refocus on what he was doing.

If someone stopped by your desk and gave you five sentences on a piece of paper and said "Please look at this 20 times a day for the next week but don't do anything with it," wouldn't you think that was crazy? Yet, that is exactly what you're doing when you leave tasks in your inbox.

Don't let that happen. Take the time, one time, to drag each email to your Task bar, write a subject line, select a due date, set a reminder for yourself and also send a reminder to the person who needs to be reminded. Then *delete the email.*

### The Calendar: personal time, meetings, appointments

An email frequently triggers the need to schedule time to work on something when you can study, concentrate or create. Don't leave that email waiting in your inbox until you plan to actually do that work. Instead, decide when you want to get started on the project, drag the email to the Calendar bar on the navigation pane and drop it there. An Appointment window will open before your eyes.

As with the Task window, the Appointment window will contain all the information in the email itself, the time, date and person who sent the email, and the same Subject line. Change the Subject line to describe what you want to do during the appointment. The window will also provide space to designate a meeting location and a space to set a start time and an end time. You can also set a reminder to pop up and type in any additional notes and thoughts above the text of the email, which you can edit while you're thinking about it. You might be planning to spend this appointment time soon or off in the future, so include any helpful information while it's fresh in your mind to make things easier when the reminder pops up.

Let's say you have a document on the hard drive of your computer that you will need during your appointment. You can insert the current version of the file and have it open for you with a double-click in the Appointment window. If you might modify the file after you schedule this time and before you will work on it, insert a hyperlink to the file instead. The hyperlink will open the latest version of the file.

If you want to set aside several blocks of time to get the job done, you can click Recurrence in the Appointment window or its equivalent in your program. The appointment recurrence window opens, offering any number of options for you to customize the use of your time.

Now suppose, after considering a received email on the second pass, you would like to call a meeting to deal with the issues triggered in your mind as you read and absorbed the content and its implications. As you did to schedule some private time for yourself, drag and drop the email onto the Calendar bar. Type the subject, time, location and reminder. Write notes to yourself and others above the email text, and add any pertinent files or hyperlinks. To invite people to your meeting, hit the Invite Attendees button, or its equivalent in your program. Add addresses of the attendees on the To line and hit Send. When people receive your invitation, they can accept or decline it. You will receive an email from each person indicating whether they accepted, declined, or are tentative. Then *delete the original email from your inbox.*

Let's give further consideration to the documents you might need for your meeting, where to keep them and how to readily access them before the meeting. You might have notes, minutes, an agenda, a slide presentation, background reading, contracts and spreadsheets. Where do you keep all this material?

Create a file folder called Meeting Material, or something like that, and insert the agenda, sales projections and whatever documentation is needed into the folder. Within the Appointment window, create a hyperlink to the Meeting Material folder. When you receive your meeting reminder, you can click the hyperlink to bring you to the material you need for your meeting. If you have lots of meetings to attend, you may need to create or refer to various folders pertaining to specific areas of work. Sales forecasting, project reviews, staff meetings. Put a hyperlink on each appointment page to identify the folders you need.

Here's another idea. Block out preparation time, personal time, project hours and travel time for yourself. If you have to walk from one location to another, drive or fly, block out that time on your calendar. Push the Calendar bar and assign the time. Manage your time before someone takes the opportunity to do it for you.

### Notes

An email arrives that has information you want and will need in the future. It could be instructions for setting the office alarm or rules for expense reporting. Does it belong in a file? Are you going to read it later? Put it on the calendar? No! You want to keep this information handy so you have it when you need it. So, just leave it in your inbox, right? No! Make it into a note by dragging it to the Note bar in the navigation pane, the note program or the equivalent on your computer.

As with tasks, appointments, and the calendar, a Note window will open on your computer screen containing all the information that's in the email. Write a name on the note that you will recognize when you want to retrieve it. When you push the Close button, the note will automatically be added to your list of notes, and you can *delete the original email.*

To recall your notes, click the Note button. Notes usually have several features: cut and paste into other documents or into an email, drag and drop back into your inbox, or convert to a task by dragging and dropping onto the Task bar in the navigation pane. In the Note window, you should also find Save, Print and Forward options.

MasteringEmail™ Examples

As a review, let's examine five sample emails arriving in your inbox that call for specific actions.

**From the boss: strategic planning**

Your boss wants figures for an upcoming strategic-planning session in three weeks. You don't have the numbers and need to talk to several people to get them. You can probably accomplish that with a few phone calls but can't work on it right now. First, you know your boss will want current, fully updated numbers; and second, the strategic-planning meeting isn't for three weeks. What is this email? It's a task. So you drag and drop it onto the Task button in the navigation pane with a reminder set for a few days before she needs the information. You also include some notes to yourself about who to contact for the information. Good! All the information you need is in the body of the task, so you can *delete that email.*

Do you have to send an email back to your boss saying you got the message and you'll take care of everything? No! Only get back to her if she has indicated that she wants you to, or if you know from experience that she likes her people to close these loops. Otherwise, assume that your boss trusts you and that you are trustworthy. No need to disturb an already busy boss with one more unnecessary email, or spend your precious time on unnecessary behavior.

### From a co-worker: agenda and report for a meeting

An email from a coworker reads, "Here are the report and agenda for the meeting on Thursday, 9:30, in conference room B." Okay, fine. You open the agenda and consider it carefully to make sure you know the items for which you have responsibility. Next, you save the agenda and the report in your Meeting Material folder. You convert the email to an appointment on your calendar by dragging the email and dropping it onto the calendar button on the navigation pane. You insert the start/stop time, reminder and conference room location. Finally, you insert, in the appointment itself, a hyperlink to the agenda and the report within your Meeting Material folder. The original email? *Delete it.* When the meeting day arrives, you simply open the appointment, click on the hyperlinks and you'll be ready for the meeting.

### From a team leader: sales meeting date change

The email tells you that the sales meeting has been moved to a different day and location. Instead of leaving it in your inbox, you depress the calendar button in the navigation pane and adjust the date and location of that appointment. You could be finished here and ready to delete the email; however, you think it might be a good idea to save the email in case anyone questions you about the change. So, cut and paste the text of the email into the body of the appointment. Now you are finished with the email and can *delete it* from your inbox.

## From a colleague: funny article about a competitor

An amusing article about a competitor arrives from a colleague. You don't have time to read the article but usually have lunch with this person, who will probably tell you about it then. So you can *delete it*. On the other hand, let's say you want to keep the article to read yourself later. Drag it to RIL. If it pertains to a project, save it to that project's folder. What have you done? You have put the email where it has meaning and can be retrieved at your convenience. In all cases, you can comfortably *remove it from your inbox*.

## From Accounting: faxing expense reports

This email contains new instructions for how to fax your expense report to the accounting department. You only do expense reports once a month and you know you'll forget the specific procedures by the next time you must do it. You certainly don't need to see it, lurking there in your inbox, every time you open up your email. So, turn it into a note by dragging and dropping it onto the Note button. Name the note Fax Expense Report Instructions, so you can easily locate it by scanning through your notes later on. Also, set a reminder. *Delete the email* and forget about expense reports until the reminder pops up.

Great job! You are mastering email. You've gone through five emails in probably less than five minutes, while efficiently organizing work and planning your time.

If you get 50 emails a day, then, doing the math here, you'll be able to process them in an hour or less. The more you practice, the faster you'll get; and the more you share this methodology with others, the fewer emails you will receive and need to process.

Are you still afraid you'll lose something if you delete the email? Let's think through a few scenarios to illustrate how your fears are misplaced. Consider our five emails again.

First, the boss calls and says the meeting got moved up a week and she needs those strategic planning figures now. No problem. "Strategic numbers for the boss" is in your task list. You scan the list, find it, open it, review your notes and contacts and you're on it.

You see an email message that changes the time and location for the meeting you established above. No problem. You go to the appointment on your calendar and update the location and time. The hyperlinks are still there to the agenda and report; you don't have to touch them. You will get a reminder at the appropriate time. *Delete the email.*

You get another email from Accounting saying that the fax number they provided in the original email is wrong; there was a typo. No problem. Open your notes, copy the new number and paste in the corrected information, and *delete the email.*

These examples looked at five email messages and three more that changed information previously received. If you were not efficient in managing your email, you'd have to open three pairs of emails to see what they said and which one was current. Which email has the right fax number? Where is that meeting; did it move or not? Multiply this by 50, 75 or 100 emails over a course of a week, or a day if you're that busy a person, and calculate how much time you'll save not having to sort through stale inbox information or do email during dinner with your family or friends.

One might argue that it takes longer to do something concrete with each email than just leave it where it is, and that's true; however, if you process it once, you're done; and you're performing actual work related to whatever is in the email, while vastly reducing the confusion, tedium, and mental fatigue that results from an overloaded inbox. Plus, as you begin to routinely convert emails into tasks, appointments, calendar entries, and notes, you'll naturally get faster and faster at it, while experiencing the satisfaction of taking care of business. You can then forget about the issues presented in your inbox and at the end of the day shut down your email and get on with your life.

# Five

# Sending an Email

Here are a number of efficient practices to follow that will benefit both you and recipients when sending, replying and forwarding messages.

First and always, think about whether sending an email is the most sensible vehicle for what you want to do. Consider face-to-face conversation, often so much better, or a phone call. What approach maximizes the chance of win/win/win communications? If the email is going to be complex, contain multiple paragraphs and involved explanations, it would absolutely be better to talk directly to the person, so you can check for understanding, clarify your meaning, hear the other person's point of view, get answers to your questions, and avoid making assumptions that will only prolong the process. Remember, you can talk faster than you can type and won't have to wait for a reply, so dialogue will often produce a favorable outcome in less time. It is hard enough to communicate; don't use email for conversations better carried on in person or by phone.

If you determine that email is the right tool, compose a concise, precise message. Don't ramble. State what you want done, by whom and by when. Attach needed documents, reference necessary files, and, when you want to include something from the web, insert a link to the exact location rather than just a reference to the material so the receiver doesn't have to hunt it down. The potential for frustration and lost time when you don't send the link is multiplied by the number of people receiving the email. If you think this approach too cumbersome or the necessary files are on paper, you still have a post office and overnight delivery at your disposal.

I write my email in two forms. If it's short, I don't separate paragraphs or double-space. Here's a single-spaced example.

September 14, 2013
Hi Jennifer:
Please get me a room at the Inn, ar Mon, Sep 24, lv Fri, Sep 28. Check with Dick and find two hours when he and I can meet on Tue.
Thanks,
Bob

Suppose Jennifer gets the room and the appointment and wants to let me know. She should be able to set up an option in her email program to reply with her name and her notes following each of my comments. That might help us keep our records straight. Her reply would look like:

**/Jen** Hi Bob
September 14, 2013
Hi Jennifer:
Please get me a room at the Inn, ar Mon, Sep 24, lv Fri, Sep 28. **/Jen** Got it!
Check with Dick and find two hours when he and I can meet together on Mon. **/Jen** 11 to 1, Friday; you'll have to buy him lunch.
Thanks,
Bob
**/Jen** Seeya soon

For longer messages with several lines per paragraph, I'd separate the paragraphs for clarity. Remember, no email should be very long, so if you can see that your message might generate a back-and-forth of questions and concerns, pick up the phone. A personal call can get all the questions and concerns resolved, avoid threads and eliminate misunderstanding.

What is a good email message length? A message with a few sentences is preferable, definitely not a lot of paragraphs. How many subjects should there be in an email? Make it one subject and put a clear description (word, phrase or short statement) on the Subject line.

Remember, you and everyone else are battling full inboxes and the time it takes to go through them. Surely, you appreciate receiving brief, to-the-point emails that you can read quickly, understand and act upon. Understand that recipients of your email feel the same. For thousands of years there was no email and everyone managed to communicate. Countries were formed, laws were made, wars were fought and business was conducted, all without email.

Be focused and direct when composing email. Don't be chatty or pour out a stream of consciousness. Make your purpose clear by asking for or saying exactly what you want. Suggest meeting dates. Set or request deadlines. Tell the recipient why you are sending information or forwarding another email. Read it over, edit for clarity and purpose and take out extra words before you hit Send. Such focus and care can avoid duplicate work, frustration and embarrassment for you or the recipient.

Give careful thought to what you put on the Subject line. Be sure it's pertinent. Your email is competing with other email for the attention of your recipient(s), so make sure the subject stands out, perhaps a statement that summarizes the message and gives your reader a good idea about what is required. And if you forward an email or reply to all, consider whether you should change the Subject line. Your Subject line might read:

- Take action please

- Need your decision on xyz by Friday

- Please respond by xyz

- FYI only—no action required

- Follow up to our meeting on xyz

- Please read—urgent issue

- xyz meeting for Tuesday CANCELLED

- xyz meeting MOVED to Wednesday

When you reply to an email, re: will appear on the Subject line with the original subject phrase. If the subject is the same, leave it. But if you are changing the subject of the communication, change the Subject line as well. If you see re: re: re: on the Subject line of a received email, you can be pretty sure the subject has changed.

Dale Carnegie's sixth human-relations habit states how important a person's name is to them. So always write a salutation, and use the person's name.

Send your message only to people who need to take action. Avoid using Reply to All casually—in fact, try not to use it at all—and avoid unnecessary carbon copies. I'm sure you've received many copies that didn't pertain to you and asked yourself why they were sent. Maybe you even got annoyed at the sender for forwarding unwelcome email.

There once was a criterion for sharing information that may function well here: the distinction between "need to know" and "want to know." If you believe the person really *needs* to know, put their name on the To line. If you believe the person might simply *like* to know, don't send it. They won't know what they're missing, and you'll reduce system overload.

It's also not a good idea to use capital letters for a whole message. It comes across as too forceful, maybe even arrogant. The reader may feel you are YELLING AT THEM. Capitalize a few words for emphasis, if you like, or italicize.

Unless it would motivate or be politically correct, eliminate sending email to say thanks, you're welcome, no problem, glad to help, get back to you later or I appreciate it. Instead, make it a common practice among colleagues with whom you normally communicate to take such replies for granted. For the occasional person who does you a favor and might think you are ungrateful, of course send a sincere thank-you. If you think someone outside the team might feel unappreciated or left out, take a moment to assuage them: maybe an email, maybe a phone call. Acknowledging a new business contact would certainly be appropriate. People do appreciate a thank you; slip it into your salutation, when you sign off, or on the Subject line, if appropriate. Always trust your instincts in the moment, as there are exceptions to every rule.

Threaded email, which contains previous messages below the sender's message, can be useful or a waste of time. If you like it, use it, but do so judiciously to avoid confusion. If your work requires keeping a history, that's the way it is. Just don't let unnecessary threads get out of hand. Threads will automatically develop when users have selected the option in their email program to include the received message when they reply or forward. Unless the individuals on your To line really need the contents of the thread, take the time to cut all or part of it, or start a new message. If you are replying to the sender, keep in mind that the sender already has the threaded information, so replying without it will be more direct. Sending the same old continuous thread to everyone, without adjusting the Subject line or reconsidering to whom you send it is thoughtless. Information might be misunderstood or even get to someone you would rather not see it. Often, just composing a new message, with a new subject, makes more sense.

In general, when forwarding, take the time to eliminate clutter. The more extraneous stuff you send, the more it detracts from your intended message and distracts the recipient(s). Key employees are often concerned about accuracy, compliance and misunderstanding, and administrative people are often afraid they might miss something they are expected to do, so they end up unnecessarily investing time to read the entire thread to make sure all is okay.

Email is not a good media for certain subjects, such as performance feedback, reprimands and double-meaning messages. It is easy for written communications to be misunderstood and for people to make assumptions that are incorrect, leading to rumors, group posturing, defensive positioning and hurt feelings. People may retreat, defend or avoid, thus diminishing their productivity and the productivity of others. Use one-on-one meetings or the telephone for these subjects so that you can see body language, hear tone of voice and, through dialogue, get a truer picture of what is meant by the words.

You may regret sending an email in haste during an emotional time, because once those words are out, the harm is done. Don't use email to criticize, condemn, complain, blame, threaten or defend. You may have seen in the news where email provided damaging evidence for the whole world to see. Email messages can be subpoenaed for you to explain. An unclear message misinterpreted by the compliance police can cause you a lot of anguish. Pay attention! Take a breath and invest a few more seconds to protect yourself and avoid the hassle.

If you do feel overcome by emotions, expressing your thoughts and feelings is a healthy way to let them out and regain your composure so you can move on. So go ahead, type your emotions out on the screen. CAPITALIZE. Underline. *Italicize.* Use as many exclamation points as you want!!! Write until you feel the urge to flop back in your chair. Then sit back with a cool head, rely on your integrity and compassion to figure out a more professional way to handle the issue, and delete what you wrote. *Do not send an emotional email.* And make sure you don't inadvertently address it and hit Send out of habit.

You probably have an option in your email program to mark your message as urgent. If the receiver has arranged their inbox according to importance, your urgent message will appear at or near the top of the list. Of course, those receiving your message may have their own opinion as to whether your email is important. Don't risk being the boy who cried wolf. If you use Urgent too much, your reader will ignore it. As a team member, manager or employee, it's best to decide together what "urgent" means and proceed accordingly.

Most programs will let you request receipts so you can know whether the email was received and/or read. These tracking options are useful in formal situations, such as following a contract or agreement, but don't add to the overload by using them for ordinary correspondence.

# To Send an Email

------------------------------------------------

Think about the appropriate mode of communication:
email, phone, text or private conversation.

Make your message concise and precise.

Edit your message carefully.

Write a meaningful subject line.

Imagine paying $1.00 for each carbon copy you send.

Imagine paying $5.00 to send a complicated history.

Reconsider.

Proofread.

Send.

# Six

# Group and Team Email

We don't usually work in a vacuum. We collaborate, share and make joint decisions in groups or teams. A group is any number of capable colleagues, accountable for their own individual results, with a casual requirement to support each other. Team members, on the other hand, believe they are all in it together, with no individual prizes. If one loses, they all lose.

How does a team use email? Given all the possibilities for misunderstandings, high-performance team members *talk* to each other, in many cases, to come to mutually satisfying conclusions—they don't rely on email. A group member should give that approach some thought. Ask yourself, is it worth my time to prepare this email, and will it be worth the recipient's time to process it?

## Carbon Copy Email

When you receive a carbon copy, the original message is directed to one or more individuals who should be required to take action or gain from that information. Why would you receive a carbon copy? Most of you in favor of cc email say it keeps you in the loop. What could that mean?

- You are a member of a team, and everyone needs to know what everyone else says and does.

- You are an administrative assistant or project manager, and you maintain the files.

- You requested a cc about a certain issue.

- You have a new hire and you want to keep tabs on what they're saying to whom.

- You were in a different time zone when an important meeting took place, so you got the information via cc email. Maybe you received minutes. (For minutes, names should appear on the To line.)

Some of you are not too happy with all the cc email you receive; what could be the reasons? Consider the following ideas.

- You didn't ask for it and don't know why it comes to you. Still, to make sure you're not missing anything, you read it, and mostly feel as if you wasted your time.

- You invest the time to read carbon copies to make sure they don't require action on your part or contain compliance violations, and mostly the investment doesn't pay off.

- You feel frustrated by one more email that confuses you, diverts your attention and wastes your time, so you just hit the Delete button, and you hit it pretty hard.

What do you do with cc email after you read it? Do you need to keep it or spend time filing it? Do you leave it in your inbox to consider later? You could decide to delete all cc email without even reading it. Some do. However, that may be too hard for you. Consider the following options:

- Scan quickly and delete.

- Read and consider. You know to whom it was sent, so, if you ever need to get involved, you can contact them. If they truly need you, they can contact you. Delete the email.

- Read and consider. You know the sender who has the information contained in the email. If you need that information someday, you can ask for it. Therefore, delete the email.

- Read and consider. If you really want to keep the email or the content and have a file for this project, subject or customer, drag it to the folder. It will be available when you need it, where you need it, and will no longer steal your attention.

- Read and consider. If it's important and you want to spend time with it later, drag it to RIL.

- If it upsets you because you can't decide what to do with it, drag the message to JGKI and move on. The darn thing will be out of the inbox and won't make you anxious every time you see it.

- Don't have time to read it now? Can't delete it because it might contain something important? Expect to get to it later? Okay. Drag it to RIL.

- Afraid to get cc mail mixed up with other reading? Establish a cc folder and move carbon copies to that folder to read when you have a chance. You will feel better about still having it available, though you will probably never do anything with it. If anyone questions you about an unread cc message, you can ask them to remind you about it.

Okay, suppose you do tuck the carbon copies away in RIL, JGKI or a cc folder. Maybe you'll get around to reading them and taking action; good. What if you look at your file and find a cc over 10 days old? Is it worth reading? If nothing has come of it in 10 days and you haven't needed the information for 10 days, this email has to be purged. Be courageous and just delete! You can also set the folder to auto-delete after a reasonable period of time.

I go back a ways with computer-systems development. Let me share some history. Before email overloaded, we had printer paper. It was customary to print reports on green and white striped paper in 132-column format and distribute copies to whomever. Almost every office you entered had a pile of these green-and-white-striped reports on a work table. People would joke about there being a room in every office complex piled to the ceiling with these records. It was generally believed that no one needed these reports or read them; yet, they piled up and were stored.

I see carbon copies as a sequel to the paper overload of yesteryear. They pile up in the inbox or get shoved into a never-to-be-read folder until someone moves, dies or goes out of business. So why do we continue to send them? Whatever the psychological reason, let's just stop it.

One time, I arranged with the manager of a key employee to hold a coaching session with that employee. In my coaching practice, after approval, the dialogue and results remain confidential between the employee and me. The manager sent me an approval email and carbon-copied her boss, the boss's admin and the employee. I then sent an email to the key employee with initial instructions, without sending any carbon copies. How long do you suppose the boss, boss's admin and employee allowed the carbon copies from the manager to linger in their inboxes, seen and thought about over and over, before they got around to deleting them?

Another idea: Set up a central file for individuals, projects, or whatever. Have the email server direct all cc mail to the appropriate file. If anyone wants to check it, they can. If anyone needs to check it, they can. Then configure the system to purge all mail that exceeds 30 days, whether read or not.

From another point of view, the presence of unnecessary carbon copies in your inbox can alert you to management, leadership or personnel challenges. Consider the following examples and solutions.

- If an employee sends you a carbon copy because they want your attention, give them appropriate attention as their manager or team mate and help them learn to operate confidently.

- If the cc is letting you know that the sender is doing the job they're supposed to do, let them know you trust them and empower them to do the job without having to notify you of their every move.

- When carbon copies are used to blame, self-defend or avoid responsibility, this is a cultural, team or personal issue. If you are directly affected, have a talk with someone who might be able to help you.

- If someone is trying to cover their tracks using carbon copies, this is a personal, team or management issue. If you can, talk to the person's manager, who is in a position to address the issue and help the individual.

- Carbon copies to a boss might indicate that the employee doesn't feel trusted, feels unsure of responsibility or is in a role that is not clear. A boss recognizing the underlying motivation can be helpful in getting it resolved.

- If someone doesn't seem to discern the difference between email directed to them and carbon-copy email, you may have a lonely, longing or isolated person in need of help.

Strive to become more conscious of the hidden messages behind some carbon copies. Addressing them can build self-esteem, trust, relationship, communications, accuracy and collaborative results.

If you're frustrated by how much time you waste reading carbon copies, consider sending a brief reply to the sender—not to everyone on the list. You might say, "I feel overloaded with email, so I prefer not to spend time on carbon copies. If you need my help, really want me to know something or expect me to take action, please put me on the To line. Thanks for your consideration." If you want to automate the process, send such a message as an auto-reply when your name is on any cc list. Using MasteringEmail principles and etiquette, you and your team can decide among yourselves the appropriate use of carbon copies.

### Threaded Email (History Files)

Threads develop when you have selected the option in your email program to include the original message when you reply or forward—a helpful feature when working on many things at once or a project that requires a history of correspondence, as it brings the last message, or history, back into mind.

You must receive some email with long threads of previous correspondence from numerous people. Ask yourself if you find that to be helpful and necessary or annoying and confusing, and take extra care to keep your own correspondence meaningful and clutter-free.

If you work in customer relations or with a virtual team, you have to handle several issues at a time and multitask various requirements for action, collaboration, delay, case work and audit trails. In most of these cases, email is your communication medium and threads are helpful or necessary.

There are other good reasons for threads. You might want to preserve the original language: foreign, scientific or medical. To avoid making transcription mistakes, you might send an email with a lot of names or numbers. Forwarding a threaded message makes sense, in another way, when you create an email dialogue that a third person wants to read for training or need-to-know. When a thread pertains to one subject and contains a complex conversation, it could be very useful to some people. Being busy, the participants could forget what has been said or who said what; by looking the details over again, they can see the picture more clearly.

Threaded email loses its value when it gets complicated or too broadly disseminated. Suppose a team member requests ideas about solving a problem from all of you on the team and many of you respond. Following that, several members send and respond to each other, all within the thread. In threaded team emails, you might read statements such as: "I already did this," "I wasn't there, but I have the information if anybody wants it," "What do I have to do with this," "Can you help me?," "Sally said there's more to this," "I met with Billy and he said Dick's approach conflicts with policy," "For your information, I read this and it is not acceptable."

These comments, in an incoming email, could peak your curiosity and lead you to read the whole threaded email again. If you were involved with your top priorities when you responded to the alert, turning your attention to the conversation would be an unnecessary distraction and a waste of time. Here is a good reason for turning off your email after you have processed a batch.

When you do a familiar job every day, using email in conjunction with regular mail, meetings and telephone conversation, why would you need to deal with a lot of history anyway? You don't record telephone conversations or meeting dialogue, do you? There is no need, usually, for sending history when you are concerned with day-to-day business operations. You, as employee or manager, must be aware of what you are doing and use email mainly to make and receive action requests.

Threaded email could contain superfluous commentary or be used for improper personal reasons—to show who's doing what to whom, point a finger at who is not doing what they should, cover one's tracks, build a case, redirect responsibility, prove something, or place blame. This behavior is not productive, it's not laudable, and it can be abusive.

### Team Email

The best way to improve your team email is to discuss it together, provide honest feedback about your experiences, and make collaborative decisions about process and content. Develop norms for sending and receiving, decide what messages are helpful and what messages hinder, agree on how to reach one another with an urgent message.

### Nominal Group Technique

Consider for a moment the Nominal Group Technique, NGT, which provides an orderly email process for communicating with a number of team members concerning a specific issue. It's effective for virtual-team problem-definition, problem-solving and decision-making. Take a look at an example.

Assume your team lead is the facilitator, attempting to solve a problem, and several members of your team, spread all over the world, are required to participate. The NGT process would work like this.

Leader's email #1:

"Here is my definition of the problem I would like you to help me solve. Please review it and send back to me what you believe is a better problem-definition."

You and each of your team members would consider the request and, individually, email what you believe to be the best definition of the problem back to the team lead. You would not reply-to-all. The team lead would analyze and synthesize all the inputs and create a new, deemed-to-be-more-accurate definition of the problem.

Leader's email #2:

"Thank you all. I have modified my definition of the problem based on your input. Here is the new problem definition. Please consider the possible causes of this problem and send me your list."

In order to make a contribution, you and your colleagues might do some personal research and communicate one-on-one with others involved in the situation. Each of you would then send an email back to the team lead (and only the team lead) listing what you believe to be possible causes of the problem.

Leader's email #3:

"Thank you for your ideas. Based on your input, I conclude there are three possible causes of this problem. Please consider the following three causes independently and send me your thoughts on each."

Using NGT, your team can communicate in an orderly fashion, working on the same issues, in short bursts, without being in the same location or meeting room. This technique allows the team leader to process all the inputs, without the team members getting biased by seeing everyone else's input. Individuals can process requests within their own time frames and time zones, and the goals of MasteringEmail are met by eliminating extraneous communication and email between team members, extraneous input sent back to the team lead, unnecessary carbon copies and unnecessary historical threads. Give it a try!

# My Idea Page

------------------------------------------------

What ideas will I implement to manage my email better?

What ideas will I promote to my team members and boss?

What benefits will I derive for myself and my family?

# Seven

# Special Applications

Let's take a brief look at special situations that will further relieve email overload.

## Emotional Email

Continuing the conversation about emotional email begun in the last chapter, you might be the recipient of such an email—blaming, threatening or venting. Don't reply to it. Delete it and simply wait. In time things will probably sort themselves out, likely with a personal request for forgiveness from the embarrassed sender. Was it a small problem for you? If so, accept the apology; forgive, forget and move on. If the message for some reason does pose a real problem, don't try to resolve anything with email.

If you are the one who has sent an email in haste during an emotional time, realize that once it's out there the harm is done. All you can do is humbly apologize as soon as you are able to. Learn from your mistake, and discipline yourself from sending future emails that criticize, condemn, complain, blame, threaten or defend. These feelings are usually better kept to yourself, vented in a journal or shared with a non-work friend, or, if truly relevant to professional matters or relationships, addressed privately with the individuals involved.

## Gossip

Suppose you're emailed an open-ended question like "What did you think of that meeting?" My take is that the sender heard or observed something about someone or some situation, usually something negative, and wants to gossip. You could shoot back an answer and start a back-and-forth with the sender; you could also just smile and wait for the phone to ring, or bring the subject up the next time you meet. Avoid generating these types of email conversations, which contribute to overload, distraction and possible embarrassment. Imagine that your gossip is forwarded to Sally with carbon copies to Tom, Dick and Harriet. A sensible rule of thumb is not to put in writing anything you wouldn't want the world to see.

## Undisclosed Recipients

On occasion, you might want to send an email to a number of people without showing who else is receiving it, or just keep the recipients' addresses private so they can't be hijacked by an undesirable mailing list.

To accomplish this, do two things in your address book: Create a contact using a fictitious name, and create a distribution list containing email addresses of those you want to reach.

The fictitious contact would have an email address; give it your own. When you use your own address, you receive a copy as proof that your email was sent. In the message you send, put the fictitious contact on the To line. If you think using "Undisclosed Recipients" as the fictitious name might upset some people, make up something that sounds functional, such as "Initial Planning Group" or "Strategic Initiative Team."

Okay now, you also need a name for the distribution list. Make up a name that makes sense to you like "My Team" or "Approval Committee." The recipients will never see it. Put the name of that distribution list in the bcc (blind carbon copy) box. If your email form shows only cc for carbon copy, click that and bcc should then appear. Each person who receives the email will see only the fictitious name on the To line and not any of the actual addresses.

## Reply to All

So he says, "It's so easy to hit the Reply-to-All button; it sure saves me time. I don't have to sort out what I want to say to whom, all I have to do is say what I want to everybody and anybody! They can figure it out. They have more time than I do."

So she says, "Who says Reply-to-All is a problem? I don't understand! Shouldn't we all share with one another?"

On a personal level, it might be nice to know what people are doing. Facebook sure makes us think so. For some people, email is the way they stay connected in their lives. They look forward to news, PowerPoint picture shows and short jokes about aging. Okay, enjoy!

From a business point of view, however, there are other considerations. Reply to All only when it's absolutely necessary for every person on the list to see your message; think ahead of time about who really needs to know what. Cut away information not pertinent to your reply or an audit trail, as everyone has the previous message anyway; and, as you should know by now, if the subject changes start a new message, and if the participants change add or remove them accordingly. Maybe send individual messages. The goal is clarity and speed of appropriate communication, not personal convenience.

I once saw a message from a salesperson to a customer-service representative, disputing why an order was rejected. The salesperson carbon-copied her manager. The customer service rep hit Reply to All and added her manager plus the finance department worker who flagged the order in the first place. The salesperson didn't like the answer. She hit Reply to All, adding her boss's boss and the customer-service rep's boss's boss. After the finance worker forwarded the email thread to the finance department manager as an FYI, the finance manager hit Reply to All with an explanation of finance policy and carbon-copied her boss. Then the salesperson added one more unnecessary email to everyone's inbox, thanking them for their help.

Isn't that ridiculous? This example involved about 30 emails and the time of eight people, most of whom should never have been involved. It is a common and sorry illustration of poor email practice and a continuing cause of email overload. I was consulting for their company at the time, so I talked with a leader on that list, who then initiated some training on email communications. I also talked to the process-owner, who used the experience to improve order-processing. The one good thing about bad email practice is the opportunity it provides to address and streamline individual and organizational performance issues.

### Sending Repetitive Email

Suppose you are required to send an email *every* month reporting sales results and you use a certain report format. Your email program should allow you to generate a standard form into which you can insert the new numbers.

Using a standard form will save time and effort, so you might want to poke around the help menu of your email program and avail yourself of that feature. Your email program will probably even let you create and store your own template for a form. When you're ready to send your monthly report, you would then call up the template, type in your variable data, put your distribution list on the To line and send it as a regular email.

### Customizing a Reply

If you receive an email with a question, you would most likely reply with an answer on your first pass through the inbox, assuming the answer was straightforward and you anticipated no misinterpretation. Does the email include information or a thread that is pertinent to your answer? If not—and as a way of allowing the individual who asked the question to focus on your answer—cut out everything from your reply, except the original question. If by chance the sender wanted to refer to that previous, now-deleted information, it can always be found in their sent-mail folder.

### Forwarding

What might you want to forward? As in the reply case above, cut anything irrelevant to the current exchange.

### Open-ended Questions

If you receive an open-ended question or request for a long answer—like "What do you think about . . ." or "Send me some ideas about what you would like to accomplish."—don't respond by email. Instead, make some notes for a discussion or organize a presentation, then email a request to meet.

### Auto Replies

You can usually set up an auto reply to received email by following a menu in your email program that lets you establish rules for incoming mail. Here are a couple of applications.

Say you find carbon-copy email a colossal pain in the neck, as I do. You might set up your program to respond to all carbon copies with an auto reply. Think of yourself as genuinely trying to be helpful, and resist the urge to be smug. An effective auto reply might say something like this:

Hi,

I received a carbon copy of an email from you today. Because I get so much email, I delete carbon copies without reading them and send this auto reply instead.

I would like to be responsive to you. If you expect me to take action, think the information may be very important to me or believe I can help you in some way, please call me at . . .

Sincerely,

Bob

Another idea is to send an auto reply when you won't be able to process your email for a while—you're out of the office for a few days, have health problems in the family, or go on vacation. Use auto reply—in this case as an "away-message"—to let people know the status of their email and not to expect you to take action immediately. You might say something like this:

To whomever:

This is an auto reply to your email, which I received today. I will be on an extended assignment from July 3rd through July 31st and unable to process my email during that time. I have prearranged to delete all incoming email while I am away and so will not see email to which I am auto-responding. If your correspondence can wait, please contact me in August. If you would like to reach me sooner, call me at . . .

My best to you,

Bob

You noticed that the out-of-office message above says you'll be deleting all incoming email while you're away. As an alternative to deleting it, you can most likely set up a way to save it to a special file or forward it to someone else. When you have time, explore your email program menus for other possibilities that might simplify your life, like setting up a file for correspondence from your team into which all their incoming email is automatically directed; you can also set up the program to automatically direct that email to the team lead or the person covering for you.

**Delivery Delay**

Sometimes you have to work on weekends or may just get motivated to get through your inbox. You will probably be responding, forwarding and setting up meetings as well as reading and deleting. Remember that your colleagues will have their Smartphones on at the soccer game or after the movies, and their devices will alert them every time you send something. Don't disturb them on the weekend. (The following weekend, they might get even.) Instead, find the delivery-delay option in your email program and schedule the delivery for the next work day.

In fact, if the email does not require their attention that soon, delay the delivery for even later in the week; that way, you won't contribute to their dread at arriving to an overflowing inbox Monday morning, filled up by coworkers who happened to get industrious over the weekend. The more considerate you can be of your colleagues' time, the more considerate they will be of yours. Set a sensible and thoughtful tone whenever you can, and people will instinctively imitate it.

### No Subject

What do you think when you get an email without a subject? Does a perhaps-profane frustrated thought flash through your mind? Does your curiosity get the best of you? If you're prone to sarcasm or would just like to have some fun with a friend, you could send an auto reply saying you deleted their email because it had no subject and therefore must not have been important. Nah, that's not nice. Just make sure you're not on the receiving end of the fun auto reply, by always including clear statements on your subject lines.

### Music

Make up rules in your email program that play special melodies when emails arrive from your lover(s) or other special people in your life.

### Creative & Focused Thinking

Continually incoming email interrupts creative and focused thinking. Yet, we enable these frequent interruptions by habitually keeping our Smartphones on and at hand. If you agree that email isn't best used as an instant-communication medium—and it is not—then don't allow your Smartphone to signal you every time a message arrives. Plan your work for the day and, after finishing your appointment with yourself to batch process your email, shut down the program and Smartphone so you can concentrate on your goals. An incoming email may delight you and send you off to celebrate. You also could lose a creative train of thought or novel solution to a problem.

James Allen, a British philosophical writer, wrote a famous little book published in 1903 called *As a Man Thinketh*, the substance of which is that as you think, so you are, and will create, and will be. Earl Nightingale, known as the Dean of Personal Development, produced a recording that sold over a million copies called *The Strangest Secret* and which said, "We become what we think about most of the time." Napoleon Hill's book, *Think and Grow Rich*, which has sold over 20 million copies and is still a best seller, famously declares, "What the mind of man can conceive and believe, it can achieve."

Be mindful of giving yourself time to think—stress-free, uninterrupted, focused time. Thinking is important to the work for which you are being paid and for remaining in charge of your own life.

### Processing a Large File of Email

Suppose you were out of the country for a few weeks and when you returned your inbox contained 500 emails. What would you do? I would put a temporary folder in my mailbox and scan through the 500 emails searching for *really important* messages to drag there. Then, with really important messages safely tucked away, I would open the inbox menu and select Delete All. Yes, Delete All. The onslaught of new messages will start soon enough and give you plenty to do. If you miss something, don't worry; it will come back somehow.

In another case, suppose you were asked by your manager to process the very full email inbox of a colleague who would be out of circulation for some reason, for some time. What to do? I'd do the same as above to create, as best I could, a file containing what I thought could be important to that colleague's boss or team lead. I would delete all carbon copies, FYIs, threads and miscellaneous material. I'd then consult with, and deliver the temporary folder to, the authority who could act on what remained.

# Reader's Conclusions

-----------------------------------------------

My plans to master email are:

I will get others to help me master email by:

I will propose the following email etiquette to my boss
and colleagues:

I will attempt to improve my work/life balance by:

# Eight

## Exploring Productivity: A Guide for Managers

If you are a member of upper management, hold a position of higher authority or have a broad sphere of influence in your organization, you're feeling the pain of social networking, Smartphones, and information overload—especially email distraction, which one British email expert has characterized as a modern addiction. Consequently, today's productivity is being sacrificed to today's email, which accounts for a disproportionate loss of creative thinking time and work/life balance, while increasing the bottom-line cost in dollars to companies.

Don't despair. Those of you who are called upon to lead and who set the tone for your organizations, often in ways you are unaware of, are in a unique position to recapture that lost creative time, lost life balance, and lost dollars by assertively taking steps to reduce the flow of email through your own company, if you choose to do so. You are holding the methodology—MasteringEmail™—in your hand.

First, let's explore what email overload is doing to the workplace and in our lives, as has been disclosed in any number of studies and articles.

In October 2011, BlackBerry's networks around the world went down and thousands lost their email service. Monica Seeley, international expert at the Mesmo Consultancy and a visiting fellow at Cass Business School, wrote an article about it at the time that was published at http://www.hrmagazine.co.uk. "The BlackBerry outage has served to highlight just how addicted and dependent we have become on our constant email fix," she wrote. "Email addiction contributes substantially to what has become the hidden disease of 21st century working life, 'email overload' and all the attendant ailments such as loss of productivity, stress and an unbalanced work/life balance."

The month before, in a front-page *Philadelphia Inquirer* article, ("Media-multitasking: It's a hit."), writer John Timpane envisioned a scenario in which millions of viewers are simultaneously watching four different, crucial, end-of-season baseball games. They have television remotes in one hand, handheld devices in the other, and they're all watching, switching, and sharing with each other as they cry and cheer—one huge, coast-to-coast, or even worldwide, sports-media community, a phenomenon interpreted by social behaviorists as the new social contract.

Probably the most well-known source of data in this field is Basex, the knowledge economy research and advisory firm in New York City. They worked with Intel, Morgan Stanley and Citrix, among others, and their findings and estimates of productivity loss can be found on many Internet sites dealing with email issues. Abstracts are available at www.basex.com, where their studies on information overload and the impact of email and technology can also be purchased. Basex and others have also formed an organization called Information Overload Research Group, which brings together research, solutions and people to help reduce the impact of information overload. (For more information, look at www.iorgforum. org.)

I did my own study, through my Philadelphia-area consulting firm, Performance Improvement Technologies, Inc. (www.pitod.com), conducting client surveys, studying newspaper and magazine articles, reviewing posts and blogs, gathering tips from email administrators and laboring over technical papers that analyzed how to solve the problem with more technology. The results added up to:

- Lost productivity due to constant distraction.

- Loss of priority focus due to interruption.

- Loss of creative thinking due to stress.

- Loss of work/life balance due to an always-on culture.

- Loss of company money due to all these factors.

Often, the stated causes are the sending of more email than is necessary, poor email processing, unrealistic expectation for an immediate reply and full-inbox anxiety— enabled and exacerbated by those ever faster and functional Smartphones. The result is an extraordinary number of hours being spent per day dealing with email at work and at home and increasing pressure from loved ones to get work and life in balance. My survey responders said they found themselves answering email at the dinner table, at their kids' soccer games and in the bathroom. Several took their Smartphones with them to bed.

Always-on workers spend the bulk of their time watching, listening, searching for and delivering large quantities of information that distract them when they are supposed to be working for you. Because emailers and texters have come to expect immediate replies, to both personal and professional messages, when alerted by their devices they interrupt whatever they're doing to read and respond; they then complain, feel, discover that they can't get anything done and that the days go by without them accomplishing anything—a multitasking craziness that threatens to swallow us all up.

In an August 4, 2011, press release, Harmon.ie, the social email software provider, presented some interesting statistics from their study of 1,140 workers in the United Kingdom.

42% remained glued to their communications devices during face-to-face meetings.

31% admitted to interrupting face-to-face meetings to answer their mobile phones.

19% stayed connected after they'd been told to disconnect.

As upper management, if you don't want to continue paying for lost productivity due to email, texting, and Google searches, if you don't want your stakeholders to get diminished returns in exchange for employees being socially satisfied, I strongly urge you to begin now to promote a corporate discipline that minimizes—dare I say prohibits?— Smartphone use in the office during working hours or at least during meetings. Determine what you would like your email policies to be, hold a few sessions to familiarize your people with them, and, most important, examine your own behavior and become a model for what you want to see in your employees.

There may also be legal implications for not getting information overload under control.

We live in a litigious society, and stored documents, including email and attachments, add exposure to potential legal claims. They can be subpoenaed during legal discovery, and this "e-discovery" has become a component in corporate litigations that can have serious financial and productivity consequences. On November 5, 2011, *The Philadelphia Inquirer* published an article about how email sent from jail by former Pennsylvania state senator Vincent Fumo was being used by prosecutors against him during his appeal. So be careful what you email; it could come back to haunt you.

"The 2006 Workplace E-mail, Instant Messaging & Blog Survey" conducted by the AMA/EPolicy Institute states that email mismanagement continues to take a hefty toll on U.S. employers—with 24% of surveyed organizations having experienced the subpoena of employee email and 15% having gone to court to battle lawsuits triggered by employee email.

Even if you have nothing to hide, legal fees and manpower costs just to review and process large email files during an e-discovery could be substantial. In one rumored case, a discharged employee left behind an email box containing 50,000 documents that had to be reviewed for legality, compliance and corporate exposure.

I am concerned for you, for all of us, and that concern was my motivation for developing the MasteringEmail methodology, which advocates a systemized practice of aggressive email deletion, while saving only necessary files and streamlined folders.

This book directly addresses three significant issues regarding email communications: reducing the volume of email that flows through your company, improving the way your people manage email; and, in this chapter, how you, as leaders, can better understand and manage effectively in current corporate cultures. The subject areas will raise your awareness of habitual and often unconscious email, and business, practices. The ultimate goal of this chapter is to help you recover lost productivity and redirect time and attention to their rightful focus on priorities and creative flow. Using this material as a guide, wasted time will decrease, dollars spent for non-productive hours will decrease, and your culture will move further in a direction of health, balance and fulfillment.

### Employees Feel the Need to be Connected All the Time

Employees, and people in general, have a natural desire to be connected in the world around them, and email enables them to enhance that connection. Abraham Maslow, the famous psychologist, positions social needs in the center of his Hierarchy of Needs. The hierarchy goes like this: Basic needs like food and shelter come first, followed by safety for self and family, followed by social contact. At that point in the hierarchy, people need to feel happily involved with others in the context of a larger group; they want to feel included and to stand out in that group as well. The power of this social need is exemplified by the explosion of social networking sites like Facebook, Twitter, LinkedIn and YouTube, the dynamic tools of our currently evolving social revolution.

The same need carries over into the business environment, where employees naturally want to feel needed, seen, and important. Some dread missing something or being left out. Isolation and loneliness are instinctively avoided, and, in an organization, they are conditions that can be experienced as downright scary.

In her article, mentioned earlier, email expert Monica Seeley wrote:

"More than 60% of the business users we surveyed felt that they must stay tethered 24x7x365 to their BlackBerry or similar device (even on Christmas day, driving and in the bedroom). When asked why, most confess that it is self-imposed, rather than their boss's (and client's) expectation."

The handheld Smartphone—in that it's a clock, a phone, a mail box, an Internet browser, a calendar and a gaming device—is the perfect tool for enabling the sense of connection identified in Maslow's hierarchy of needs. It is changing our world, mostly for the best, perhaps. Yet what do we do about the associated productivity losses and impact on home life that result from this growing need to always be *on*?

The MasteringEmail methodology calls for processing email only during specific prearranged appointments during the day and shutting email down in between. It instructs you forcefully to shut your Smartphone off during meetings. Well, even if I promise myself not to process email all the time and to check for phone messages only between meetings, every time I glance at my device I see more work ahead that I'm tempted to dispatch at that moment whether it makes sense to do so or not. The device is on me wherever I go, all day and all night, flashing, gonging, beeping, buzzing, and alerting me to every single incoming email, text, or update. Who can resist? I start to ask myself, do I need a real phone, a land line? It's only a matter of time before people won't even know what a land line is. Do I even need to wear a watch? The issue is complicated and requires upper management to start thinking about the processing of information as a priority task. Take a look at two scenarios.

**Scenario #1**: I have my Smartphone with me in your staff meeting with the sound off. I check it once in a while for the time, like looking at a watch, but when I do I also notice that an email has arrived and my mind takes off. Is it the boss? Is there something wrong at home? Does somebody need me? Am I in trouble? So, I check the email sneakily on my lap, and now I'm concentrating on that and not listening to you. The result: loss of meeting communication, priority focus and time. This scenario may seem banal to you, as it has become such an ordinary and pervasive practice; it may seem minor. But you only have to multiply it by the numbers of employees, meetings, and incoming emails to appreciate the insidious way in which the Smartphone is cutting into your business.

**Scenario #2:** Suppose I make it through your meeting without looking at my Smartphone. After the meeting, I'm so anxious to see if anybody has contacted me that I avoid getting into any follow-up conversations that might actually be relevant to my work priorities. I look at my Smartphone and see several messages; I'm curious, so I open my email. Distracted, I'm late for the next meeting. I also leave that email in my inbox, because I don't have time to process it there and may need other tools than my Smartphone to do it; instead of dealing with it fully, I'm going to have to look at it again later. Or perhaps I actually did look at my Smartphone during the meeting—just once, real fast, when the email came in—and I shot off a quick reply when I should have been paying attention, and now I'm worried that my hastily composed answer may have confused the recipient. I also wish I had taken time to hit the restroom. The result: productivity loss, anxiety and physical discomfort.

To eliminate these problems, I'm calling on you to begin addressing the issue now, today. *Make it a priority.* Observe, analyze, discuss. Figure out what is happening with the information flow and Smartphone usage in your unique environment with your unique employees, how it's affecting productivity and the workplace culture. Set some norms and stick to them.

Resolve to train and support your people in processing email only at their desks during regular appointed times, returning calls around lunchtime and taking a final run through inboxes at the end of the day. It's one of those things that is simple but not easy, as it requires discipline, even courage. I do realize that key employees often need to use their Smartphones for their calendar, checking and making appointments throughout the day as they move about the organization. There can be exceptions to rules, as long as everyone knows and understands what they are and why.

Some high-tech spokespersons acknowledge that they have created the beast and are trying to tame it with more technology and artificial intelligence. We now have airplane mode, and new applications come out every day. In the meantime, Smartphones are getting smarter and faster, and communications companies are shoving new, better, faster networks down our throats. Perhaps your managers can give more thought to using the right technology at the right time.

Personally, I had my watch fixed and now wear it when I am with clients. I've exchanged my Smartphone for a cellphone, so I'm not distracted but can be reached when it is important. And, when I travel, I look at my email morning and evening on an iPad, using my hotel WiFi or, during flight delays, the airport WiFi, and I can watch downloaded movies on my iPad after a hard week on long flights back to Philly.

## Corporate Culture Sets Performance Expectations

Upper management manifests the corporate culture. Your expectations are met by the people below you. Consider psychologist B.F. Skinner's behavior-modification therapy, which holds that people will respond predictably to stimuli. Behaviors you reinforce happen more often, and what you don't like to see happen and don't reward will diminish. What do you reward? What do you ignore? Consider how the expectations you hold for your people contributes to email overload, productivity loss and work/ life imbalance. Examine how you, yourself, are handling information overload. What example are you setting without saying a word? In my confidential coaching of key employees, I hear a lot of things. Below are examples of how some employees interpret the messages of upper management.

You better be kept in the loop, because not knowing when asked could cost you your job.

Check with a lot of people before you make a decision, because making a mistake or being non-compliant could mean your dismissal.

Take on everything thrown at you. Saying "no" could mean professional suicide.

Read everything, and go to all the meetings. You don't want to miss something and be held accountable for it later.

Email communication helps you to be seen, it gives you a presence in the organization, shows you are working, involved, a team player and earning your salary. Put in your two cents, even if you're not directly involved.

Collaborate, listen to top management and get approvals before you make decisions. You don't want to be blindsided and have your decisions overturned.

Be careful what you put in an email or say in a meeting. Others could challenge it and make you look bad.

Knowledge workers are responsible for being "on" all the time. That includes checking email at night and on weekends at the expense of work/life balance, but your family should appreciate that paycheck.

What is your culture? Do you expect your employees to respond to every email as it arrives, even in meetings with you? Do you want them to be "on" all the time, processing email nights and weekends? Should they rely on carbon copies and Reply to All to keep everyone in the loop? Perpetuate email threads to make sure they're covered if things go wrong? Run from meeting to meeting with no time to think, create, hit the restroom or grab a cup of coffee? Whatever behavior you reinforce—or whatever behavior becomes habitual that you don't do something about even if you don't necessarily want it—becomes the norm.

I believe we spend more time sorting and throwing away information than we do comprehending and integrating it. I think we are so afraid of missing something or being wrong, we miss the forest for the trees.

In a Newsweek article February 27, 2011, Sharon Begley wrote that the availability of enormous amounts of information, and the rate at which it bombards us, actually freezes our brains and sabotages our decision-making. The overload keeps information at the conscious level and disables the power of the subconscious to mull things over, and it's the combination of conscious thought and subconscious activity that leads to real understanding and creative, sharp decisions.

The conclusions in her article mirrored my own: cut down the amount of information flow by sending less email, process email in batches and shut off your Smartphone.

To find out more about the culture in your organization and its impact on email and loss, put your ear to the ground. You may hear comments such as the ones I hear from my clients. Cultural norms can and do change, either implicitly by observation, testing, reward and punishment, or explicitly through top-down planning and education. After giving thought to the culture you create and increasing your awareness of the impact it has on your people and their productivity, you will see alternatives to the expectations you set and the results achieved by them. You have the power to make changes, if you choose to do so.

## Poor Email Processing Costs Your Company Money

Lost time is lost money! Distraction and interruption steal productive time, which costs money. Loss of employee focus wastes team time, delays decisions and costs money. Lack of creative thinking time costs money. What does poor email practice cost your company in dollars? The estimates in the literature vary significantly, but most fall in the hundreds of millions of dollars.

Basex developed a web-based calculator to estimate the financial impact on organizations of information overload. I ran several examples for the given categories: Banking/ Financial Services, Healthcare, Energy/Utilities. The results came out about the same, using the following estimate of skill level in the organization (the parameters for the calculator): Highly skilled: 40%, multiple skills: 40%, single skill: 15% and non-skilled: 5%. For a company with 200 employees, the financial loss was estimated to be two to three million dollars per year. For a company with 500 employees, the loss was five to seven million dollars per year. For 1,000 employees, ten to fifteen million. For 5,000 employees, fifty-three to seventy-five million. Significant numbers. You can find the calculator, available free of charge, at www.iocalculator.com. Give it a try; run your own numbers.

In a Basex report entitled "Intel's War on Information Overload," Basex states that Intel's own research indicated that knowledge workers lost about eight hours a week due to information overload, which for a company the size of Intel would cost about one billion dollars per year. Of particular interest to me in my mission to eliminate email overload: Intel's internal surveys in 2006 revealed that the typical employee received 50-100 email messages per day, spent an average of 20 hours per week doing email, 30% of which was found to be unnecessary. Top executives received up to 300 messages per day.

To help you further examine causes of productivity loss and dollar cost, I have prepared several examples in the next section. If you are already convinced and ready to recover the losses, just skip ahead to **Poor Email Management Can Highlight Employee Performance Issues.**

### Calculating Loss of Time and Money

Let's say, hypothetically, that the burdened pay in a typical knowledge worker organization varies from $40k a year to $120k a year, averaging $80k a year, which could be a low estimate. Assume a work year at 50 weeks x 40 hours = 2,000 hours per year. The company pays $40 an hour on average. Let's try to estimate the cost per year of poor email management. The final numbers may not be exact, but just giving consideration to the numbers will demonstrate the scope and cost of email overload.

Some employees and managers spend too much time continually processing email because their email screen is on all the time. Suppose the practice of checking and processing email two or three times per day could save an individual one-half hour of intermittent processing time per day, eliminate the interruption to focused thinking and facilitate continuation with efforts that are productive. How many hours of productive time would a company with 1,000 employees recover?

500 hrs/day x 250 days/yr = 125,000 hours/yr! At an average cost of $40/hr, that time is worth $5,000,000 to the company.

Studies suggest that employees actually waste more than an hour per day on extraneous, distracting email processing. So let's suppose the 1,000-employee company could retrieve one hour/day/employee. The company would recover 250,000 hours of productive time. That would be worth $10,000,000 to the company at $40/hr. Considering an employee works 2,000 hrs/yr, 250,000 hours equates to 125 employees. If you had 125 fewer employees, the $10,000,000 saving would flow to profit. Looking at it another way, wasting 1 hr/day is wasting 12.5% of each day; that's a lot. A company with 500 employees could see a $5,000,000 loss. With 5000 employees, there would be a $50,000,000 cost for disruption, distraction and poor email practice.

Some employees use email as a ToDo list, losing concentration on the job in front of them to process every email as it arrives. Suppose an employee is interrupted by an incoming email 30 times per day. Imagine they read and consider the email, think about the message, compose a reply and send it off. That's about a five-minute job. Then they have to invest time (one minute, two or three?) to refocus on what they were doing. Those last minutes represent lost productivity. Put yourself in that position. After handling the email, you might even feel like you need a break before getting back to what you were doing.

In the example above, suppose half of those who received the message replied with a polite "thank you very much." Our example employees would look again as each one arrived, causing another interruption and another minute each time to regain their concentration on what they were doing. The "thank you," which my methodology shows to be an unnecessary practice, would cost your company more money. Add "you're welcome" or "no problem" and you can just double the figure. Very polite employees can cost you millions.

Now let's consider what it costs your company for employees to deal with 20 carbon copies per day that mean nothing to them and require no action from them. Most people can't just delete a cc, as it just might contain something important and they are social and curious. They read, consider, delete, file or leave in the inbox. Assume only a minute is required to recover from a cc. The cost: millions.

How about what it costs for an employee to deal with a threaded email that is convoluted with mixed subjects and unnecessary detail? Assume half of the 10 threaded emails received each day by an average employee were messy and meant nothing to the receiver. Figure they spent time trying to sort out the subject and what was required of them. Assume it took three minutes to read, follow the thread, check, think and delete, and another couple minutes to refocus. Millions of dollars spent for unproductive time that could be eliminated if your people carefully managed threads.

Cut the estimates in half if you like. That's still a lot of money! When employees use MasteringEmail, hours of time are saved by reducing wasted email processing. Those hours and the recovered millions from productivity loss can be put into creative service for your company. Practicing MasteringEmail will also mean more free time for your people—less stress, higher morale and happier families. And your stakeholders will love you.

## Poor Email Management Can Highlight Employee Performance Issues

Your managers are responsible for obtaining the best performance possible from their employees. Analyzing email practice can help them do two things for you: 1) identify employee performance issues and manage the opportunity to change employee email behavior, and 2) recover non-productive hours and improve business results.

The following paragraphs explore employee performance issues that may be revealed through poor email practice. If you are already convinced that analyzing employee email practice can improve productivity and performance, feel free to skip to **In Conclusion.**

Larger companies advise workers not to use their business email for personal correspondence. They suggest, as does MasteringEmail, that they create at least two addresses. If a company does allow employees to use a single address for business and personal email, the mailbox should contain a personal folder to which personal messages can be moved and read outside the office.

You can assume, however, whatever the company rule, that individuals will check personal email during working hours—maybe just a few minutes here and there. Take an example of three minutes, four times per day. That's 12,000 minutes for a company with 1,000 employees, equivalent to a 25 head count. Opening videos and watching dramatic landscape slide shows takes much longer. Managers observing this can simply reaffirm company policy.

Let's check out Paul. He directs his attention to every incoming email. He opens it, glances, ponders, moves on through old emails, goes back, rereads, re-ponders and leaves it in his inbox for later when he has more time.

He is continually distracted from focus on priority. When Paul complains to his manager about email overload, your manager has the opportunity to help Paul change behavior, relieve the burden and achieve more focus.

John forwards to all a threaded email with a message, to prove he was not to blame for a problem. Jane replies to all with a message that makes John look foolish. Harry adds to all that he doesn't want to be a part of this conversation. Sally adds everyone's supervisor to the cc list to let them know what's going on. Your manager, receiving the cc and observing the finger-pointing, covering tracks and avoiding responsibility, can use the email thread to analyze, address and resolve performance, process, team and interpersonal issues. The threads can be a way for managers to eavesdrop on their employees' office behavior with the idea of helping them and improving the workplace.

Your manager receives a carbon copy, reads it and wonders why it was sent to her. She thinks Sam is unnecessarily escalating an issue to get attention. Does Sam think he is not trusted? Maybe Sam is just not sure who needs to know. Your manager can evaluate the use of carbon copies for effectiveness and educate people, clarify their roles and define responsibilities.

Your manager meets with Marsha and she continually refers to her email throughout the meeting. A tone chimes each time an email arrives and Marsha glances at the message. For sure, her mind changes as she reads it. Both Marsha and your manager have been interrupted and distracted; it will take time for them to refocus. With constant interruption and distraction, Marsha cannot focus on her scheduled work. Your manager can explain why email has to be shut down during all meetings.

Continually checking email throughout the day contributes to Shirley's full inbox. She is alerted to a new email, stops what she's doing and reads it. After spending time on consideration, she decides to work on it later. The next time an email arrives, she looks again, not only at the incoming message but also at older messages. The inbox fills up. Each time she looks at a new email, she is tempted to work on it. Some make her anxious. Email from her manager peaks her curiosity. In all cases, Shirley is not focusing on her work and her email behavior affects her productivity. Her manager, if aware of Shirley's full inbox, can discuss how email processing at specific times can enable Shirley to give full attention to each email. Learning MasteringEmail, Shirley will read, file, schedule time, make appointments, take notes—and remove email from her inbox.

Bill views his inbox as his priority. He pounces on each email, believing himself to be thereby responsive and spontaneous. Is that the best use of his time? Does he have enough to do? Perhaps he works on his personal business and responds to every email to indicate he is on company business. When your managers observe spontaneous email response, they have the opportunity to discuss it, resolve issues, improve productivity and, probably, improve job satisfaction.

Email communications are complicated and costly when individuals send too many messages, include too many people with carbon copies, are not careful with threaded messages and have a habit of replying to all. When your managers notice and think about the complications, they can plan to hold a MasteringEmail discussion with their people.

One survey question in an email improvement class was "How would you feel if you took care of all your email and had an empty inbox?" The responses fell into two main categories. In the first, the answers were "great," "free," "relaxed" and "wonderful." In the second, "Like my job was at risk" and "Like I was missing something." A follow-up produced comments like, "A full inbox shows how important I am," "Email indicates I am connected and a key contributor" and "I like to know what's going on: email keeps me in the loop." These attitudes generate unnecessary email, small talk and cc email, which wastes company time and contributes to the full inbox. From a management point of view, these attitudes may indicate email is serving as a way for the employee to avoid isolation, seek attention or prove to somebody, for some reason, that they are "working." There is an opportunity here for your managers to explore the employee's motivation during periodic one-on-one meetings, which can lead a happier worker who's more productive.

Some individuals cc their boss when performing everyday tasks; one extra email to process. In one observed case, I saw an employee carbon copy three layers of management in the sending department as well as three in the receiving department. Six unnecessary emails had to be processed—and this example led to complicated threads. By examining mixed-up threaded messages, your manager can clarify job requirements, information sharing and when to take an issue to a higher authority.

It is proper business etiquette to make appointments with individuals, not to be disruptive, and to meet job obligations on time. And while it is appropriate to expect a timely response, it is not reasonable to expect that a colleague be available the moment you email them, phone them or walk to their cubicle. However, more and more, the use of email increases the expectation of an immediate response, especially with managers and knowledge workers using Smartphones as their watch, telephone and calendar, in addition to web browser and email client. Your managers have to talk with their employees to define the culture and establish appropriate expectations.

Performance on the part of your knowledge workers and managers includes being creative. Creativity requires a relaxed mind, opportunity to ponder, time to read and creative conversations. When your employees say their days are crazy and they work well past six o'clock every night, they are often going home stressed out. That affects creative time and family life. If they check email at night at home, where is the work/life balance? How well do they sleep? Creativity requires a rested person who's had a good night's sleep, an uncluttered mind and opportunities to relax and think. Continual email processing at night and multitasking during family time is counterproductive. Consider the culture you create, by what you say, what you do, what you yourself are modeling.

Examine role clarity, responsibility and authority to identify redundant work, indecisiveness and the email flurry that goes with it. Clear expectations reduce employee fear, defensiveness and distress, leave more time for relaxation and creative thinking, improve productivity and work/life balance and reduce the flow of cover-up and carbon-copy email.

I'm sure you can see from these examples that your managers can directly improve performance by deliberately increasing their awareness of what's going on with their employees' email behavior. Correlating email conversations to performance issues and addressing observed situations can improve productivity and job satisfaction.

## In Conclusion

Corporate culture, technology, information overload, and the social needs of your employees effect workplace behaviors, productivity, payroll and corporate profit. By rethinking the culture you, as leadership, create, by eliminating the disruptive nature of poor email management, and by taking steps to understand the social networking revolution, you can recoup productivity and creativity losses—and the dollar cost of those losses to your company.

While you and your team develop strategies to deal with this complex environment, MasteringEmail™, available now, can help you attack a significant part of your problem. You might want to provide a book to each of your managers. Most important, set the tone yourself and your managers will follow your lead. Start by processing email in a batch, two or three times a day—as the COO of Facebook, Sheryl Sandberg, reportedly does. If you would like my support on your journey, I can run workshops to help with the transition, customized to the needs of your organization. Workshops would address both email mastery and employee performance issues revealed through poor email communications.

The sooner you begin, the sooner your workforce will start focusing less on email and more on the professional work at which you expect them to excel. The result: happier employees who get their work done on time, savings in thousands of hours and millions of dollars, and a calm and productive corporate culture.

# Appendix

# Mastering Email™ At-A-Glance

### Maintain Separate Work and Personal Mailboxes

At work, focus on your work. Attend to personal messages when you are off the clock.

### Do Not Surrender Today's Plans to Today's Email

Minimize distraction and lost time by working your plan for the day. Email is not a priority.

### Use Administrative Assistance

Trust an assistant to manage your relieve your email burden. Receive only messages requiring your personal attention.

### Batch Process Email by Appointment with Yourself

Invest less time and be more productive by planning daily, undisturbed, periods to concentrate only on doing email.

### Do Email Last In, First Serve

The most recent email will contain the latest information you need and alert you to urgent issues.

### Make Three Deliberate Passes

Scan the inbox for anything requiring immediate attention. Pass again to process quickly and respond to the needs of colleagues. Third, dwell on messages requiring more thought and concentration.

### Delete Aggressively

Act, file and delete! Don't leave email in your inbox to clutter your mind and your life. When in doubt, get rid of it.

### Send Very Few Carbon Copies

They need to know? Put their names on the To line. Nice for them to know? Don't send it.

### Send Less Email

Use email to get things done—no more Thank-you, No problem, FYI, CYA or small talk.

### Cut the Thread

Eliminate histories unless they are essential. Unnecessary threaded information wastes time, adds confusion and is frustrating.

### Empty Your Inbox Every Day

After you take appropriate action on an email, you do not need to keep it. Act decisively and empty your inbox.

### Shut Off, or Ignore, Email Alerts

Process your email according to plan. Don't allow email alerts to interrupt your work and your focus.

# About the Author

Bob O'Hare,
MSc, BSEE

Bob, as an engineer and computer scientist, developed computer communication systems and one of the first personal computers. After that career in digital technology, Bob did postgraduate work in organization development and founded Performance Improvement Technologies,

Inc. With this company, Bob facilitates corporate change, coaches executives and provides professional development services. He emphasizes the human side of leadership.

Concern by professionals and management about information overload, excess email, and productivity loss encouraged Bob to seek a solution for these issues. He researched the field and developed the MasteringEmail™ methodology to help knowledge workers, professionals and managers achieve the benefits of email without the burden. Bob wrote chapter eight of the book especially for upper management, to help them explore productivity issues that cost corporations millions of dollars annually.

To help companies change email culture and apply the MasteringEmail™ principles, Bob designs and facilitates workshops and coaching sessions to meet their needs.

Bob and his wife, Carol, two married children and three grandchildren, live and work in the Philadelphia area.

# Buy Books

Single copies of *Unload Email Overload*—and bulk orders for company leaders who would like to equip their managers with these ideas—are available at:

## www.mastering-email.com

# Free Poster

For a free, 8 ½ x 11 color poster of MasteringEmail™ At-A-Glance, visit:

## www.mastering-email.com

# Schedule a Workshop

Schedule a workshop, customized to the needs of your organization. Typical subjects include mastering email, time management, leadership development, coaching, performance improvement and interpersonal relations. Go to:

## www.mastering-email.com